IBSEN'S PEER GYNT

Ibsen's
Peer Gynt

AMERICAN VERSION

by

Paul Green

SAMUEL FRENCH

25 WEST 45th ST.   NEW YORK 19
7623 SUNSET BLVD.   HOLLYWOOD 46
LONDON - TORONTO

PRINTED IN THE UNITED STATES OF AMERICA
BY THE VAIL-BALLOU PRESS, INC., BINGHAMTON, N. Y.

FOR

Cheryl Crawford

Paul Green's American version of *Peer Gynt* was first produced in the 1950–51 ANTA Play Series by Cheryl Crawford in association with R. L. Stevens at the ANTA Theatre the evening of January 28, 1951. The production was directed by Lee Strasberg and choreographed by Valerie Bettis, setting and lighting by Donald Oenslager, costumes by Rose Bogdanoff, music score and direction by Lan Adomian. The cast of the play in the order of appearance was as follows:

AASE, a peasant widow..............*Mildred Dunnock*
PEER GYNT, her son...................*John Garfield*
AN ELDERLY MAN.....................*Ray Gordon*
AN ELDERLY WOMAN...................*Ann Boley*
ASLAK, a smith......................*John Randolph*
SOLVEIG, a neighboring girl...............*Pearl Lang*
HER FATHER, a minister..............*Joseph Anthony*
HER MOTHER..........................*Anne Hegira*
A BUTTONMOLDER......................*Karl Malden*
INGRID, the bride ....*Rebecca Darke*
HER FATHER, a farmer............ ..*Nehemia Persoff*
HER MOTHER........................*Peggy Meredith*
MADS MOEN, her betrothed.............*Mahlon Naill*
HIS FATHER........................*Edward Binns*
HIS MOTHER ....*Lisa Baker*
THE MASTER COOK.....................*Ray Gordon*
1ST HERD GIRL.......................*Lucille Patton*
2ND HERD GIRL.......................*Barbara Gaye*
3RD HERD GIRL...................*Beverlee Bozeman*
A GREENCLAD WOMAN.................*Sherry Britton*

THE TROLL KING................... *Nehemia Persoff*
THE UGLY BRAT....................... *Ed Horner*
THE VOICE........................ *John Randolph*
KARI, a neighboring peasant woman........ *Lisa Baker*
MONSIEUR BALLON.................. *Joseph Anthony*
HERR VON EBERKOPF................. *Edward Binns*
MR. COTTON....................... *Richard Purdy*
HERR TRUMPETERSTRAALE............. *John Randolph*
THE FLUTIST........................... *Hillel*
A THIEF............................ *Ray Gordon*
A HEELER........................... *Ed Horner*
A SINGER.............................. *Aviva*
ANITRA, daughter of a Bedouin chief .... *Sono Osato*
ANITRA'S ATTENDANTS................ *Patricia Birsh,*
    Barbara Gaye, Bob Emmett, Stuart Hodes
DR. BEGRIFFENFELDT, director of an
    insane asylum in Cairo............. *Joseph Anthony*
HUSSEIN, an eastern diplomat .... *Richard Purdy*
WEDDING GUESTS, TROLLS, INMATES,
    MOURNERS......................... *Lisa Baker,*
    Patricia Birsh, Ann Boley, Beverlee Bozeman, Re-
    becca Darke, Margaret Feury, Barbara Gaye, Anne
    Hegira, Peggy Meredith, Lucille Patton, Edward
    Binns, Irving Burton, Bob Emmett, Ray Gordon,
    Stuart Hodes, Ed Horner, Mahlon Naill, Richard
    Purdy, John Randolph, Lou Yetter
DANCERS....................... *Beverlee Bozeman,*
    Patricia Birsh, Barbara Gaye, Lucille Patton, Irving
    Burton, Bob Emmett, Stuart Hodes, Lou Yetter

TIME

The middle and latter part
of the 19th century

PLACE

Norway and Northern Africa

PART ONE

Scene I

A hillside by the Gynt farm. It is a hot summer day. Unseen off at the left rear is the little farmhouse. Across the middle background runs a low rail fence. A mountain path goes alongside the fence just beyond it. The heavy branch of a green tree sags down into the scene from above, marking off and emphasizing somewhat the vast and breathtaking view of the snow-capped mountains across the valley in the distance. The level foreground is framed on either side of the proscenium arch by projecting boulders or rocks in shadow. These remain throughout the entire play, enclosing each scene in something of a unit set.

When the lights go down to half-dim in the theatre, a wildly lonesome and legato Norwegian mountain folksong, played by a flute or oboe, begins behind the curtain. It is such music as a plaintive shepherd lad, high on a hill, might make as he sat gazing into the vast void of mountain valleys at the dying of the day.

The music comes nearer, and then as the lights in the auditorium hold, it recedes into the dis-

3

stance. Church bells begin ringing. They too
surge and fade as the lights dim finally out.
The curtain goes up. The shrill voice of a
woman is heard off the stage at the left rear.
AASE GYNT *is scolding her son* PEER.

AASE'S VOICE. [*Echoing in the air.*] You are lying again,
Peer.

PEER'S VOICE. [*Echoing likewise, sulkily.*] I am not
either.

AASE'S VOICE. Swear it's true then.

[*The church bells have died out.*]

PEER'S VOICE. [*Now coming near, teasingly.*] Why
should I swear?

AASE'S VOICE. [*Angrily.*] Ah-hah! You don't dare. You
are telling another pack of lies.

PEER'S VOICE. [*Crowingly.*] Every blessed word of it's
gospel truth.

[PEER GYNT *comes in from behind the little house, being*
shooed along by his mother, who grips a basket of
clothes under her arm. PEER *is a strongly built lad of*
twenty years or so, poorly dressed, unkempt and bushy-
headed. AASE, *his mother, is a middle-aged woman,*
small and delicate but obviously toil-worn. She is car-
rying a basket of clothes balanced against her hip and is
peppery with anger. PEER *is nonchalant and even a little*
morose before her abuse. She gestures him over to the
right where an axe is leaning against a rock ledge, sig-
nifying that he should get to work cutting wood. PEER
shies around her and stands grinning provokingly as he

picks up the axe and twirls it lightly and dexterously in his hands.]

AASE. [*Stormingly.*] Loafing around in the mountains a whole month long! Think of it! And it's here in the busy season too. [*Banging at the clothes.*] Tracking a reindeer in the hills, you say! And you come dragging home with your clothes torn and your skin full of briers. And where's your gun? Where's the game! And you've got the gall to ask me to believe your story. Lies! Lies! [*Peering up at him.*] Well—where did you meet this reindeer, then?

PEER. [*With a vast boyish gesture.*] West there on Gendin ridge.

AASE. [*Shivers at the mention of the ridge and breaks into scornful laughter.*] Oh, no doubt you did!

[*She begins dipping her clothes into the unseen water, scrubbing and beating them with a paddle.* PEER *stands looking up into the tree that shades the scene. A little bird has begun to sing. He answers the bird back with a fluty whistle. The bird answers him. For an instant there is a communion between them. They seem to understand each other. Then in a spirit of devilment or perversity, he steps forward, picks up a stone and pantomimes throwing it at the bird, making his whistle raucous and frightening. The bird is silent. It has flown away.* PEER *turns toward his mother.*]

PEER. It was in an alder thicket digging moss from the snow.

AASE. [*Scornfully as before, working away at her clothes.*] Oh, yes—oh, yes. [*She bangs with her paddle again.*]

PEER. [*With a mimic expression, his eyes screwed up.*]
I slid along flat on my belly, sneaking up to see him good.
Such a buck, so sleek and fat, you've never seen in all
your life. [*As if looking directly at the buck, he now lifts
his axe handle before him, sighting along it like the barrel of a gun.*]

AASE. No!

PEER. Yes. [*Loudly.*] Then—bang! [*He pronounces
the word with a "bang," simulating the firing of his gun.
AASE jumps with a squeal. PEER lowers the axe, laughing.*] I dropped him in his tracks, and then I was on him
quick as a flash. I grabbed his big hairy ear and pulled
out my knife to souse it deep in the base of his skull.
[*With a cry.*] Hey! The devil squealed like a man and
jumped to his feet. My knife went flying out of my hand.
With me hanging on a-straddle of him that buck started
running like the wind and leaping toward the ridge.

[*So intensely does PEER relive the scene that AASE stops
her washing and listens breathlessly. He moves fiercely
over toward her—the entranced and demonic hunter
riding for his life on the back of a great antediluvian
nightmare creature—through mists and snow and eerie
lands.*

*He makes a running leap by AASE, over her, as he acts
out the scene. AASE is caught in the dramatic recital. And
stranger still—except that PEER is PEER—he himself is
caught in it. And strangest of all, the scene itself is affected by his lyrical and imaginative recounting—the
lights responding to the changing mood. The elements
of wind and weather all become affected now, showing
their sympathy to the boyish braggart. The sky has*

*darkened, a rumble of thunder, a wink of lightning in
the valley.* PEER *stands on the ledge now at the back, in
tune with the infinite, his ego idem with the earth and
sky.*]

AASE. [*Involuntarily.*] Jesus save us!

PEER. Gendin Ridge is a fearsome place all right. Three
miles long and sharp as a scythe blade. Landslide slopes
and glaciers and gorges downward. The water thirteen
hundred feet below. Whee-oo! What a horse to ride!
[*He spins about the edge of the ledge.* AASE *watches him
fascinated, and sways back and forth in anxiety. She
puts out her hand supplicatingly toward* PEER *as he goes
on with his story, the air itself around him warmed to
the fervor of his imagining.*] Through the wind and
clouds we flew. And the stars all dazzling in the sky
about us. Big as lantern lights they were!

AASE. [*Murmuring.*] Peer—Peer—

PEER. Lord, we were really whizzing! And out of the
swash of foam I saw the fairies leaping. I saw them
leaping and singing and dancing about.

AASE. [*Dizzily.*] God help us.

PEER. Then a whopping eagle flew right up in the reindeer's face. He jumped as high as the house, the buck
did. And over he went into the chasm with the both of
us. [AASE *staggers to her feet and catches onto a big rock
for support.* PEER *sees her growing terror with joy. His
intensity of fervid truth increases.*] Down, down. We
fell like a rock through clouds of fog and flocks of gulls,
splitting them wide open. Down we fell, falling, like a
train running away down the mountainside. [*He imi-*

*tates the whistle of a train. The whistling echoes among
the mountains in the distance, and a flash of lightning
across the valley might be a sudden vomiting of fire from
the smokestack of the invisible locomotive.* PEER *leans far
over the ledge, suddenly fascinated by something he
seems to see below him.*] And in the black waters below
us now I see the reindeer's belly shining. It's our reflec-
tion, Mother, tearing up to meet us as we fall.

AASE. [*Gasping.*] Peer! God help me!

PEER. [*With fierce earnestness.*] And the buck falling
from the air and the buck flying up from the bottom of
the water—[*He holds his two open hands apart.*]—they
butted one another head-on—at the same second—
wham! [*He hits the palms of his hands together with a
loud crack.*]

AASE. Oh! Oh!

PEER. Whee! Did the water churn and roar!

AASE. [*Wagging her head.*] And it didn't kill you—oh,
oh.

[PEER *pirouettes around on his heels and stands still,
gazing at his mother, his lips puckered, his eyes merry
and glistening. The mood of his recital begins to pass
away from the earth and sky. The sun shines brightly
again and the sound of the wind in the valley fades away.*]

PEER. Then we lay and rested and splashed about. [*Coming nonchalantly over to his mother.*] After a while we
swam to the shore—the buck in front and me pulling
along behind. [*Gazing at his mother quizzically.*] Then
I came on home.

AASE. And you didn't break your neck. [*Lifting her eyes piously.*] Thank you, merciful Jesus! [*She reaches out and begins to feel* PEER *in a splurge of mother love.*] Oh, Father in heaven, I bless you. [*She falls on her knees as she hugs* PEER *around the legs, lifting her eyes to heaven.*] I prayed and I prayed and you answered me. My boy is safe. You kept him safe! [*Pushing away at arm's length from* PEER *and staring at him lovingly.*] It's God's mercy, son, preserved you. [*Shuddering again.*] What a terrible leap over the cliff! Think of it! [*Breathlessly.*] Thirteen hundred feet! [*Fondling him.*] Your torn britches don't matter, nor the briers. Now you are home again—safe at home. [*She rises weakly to her feet, then stops.*] But what about the reindeer—what happened to him?

PEER. [*Lets out a mocking chuckle, grabs up his axe and twirls it lightly in his hand.*] Oh, he's probably loose in the mountains somewhere. [*Measuring a tall imaginary tree with his eye, spitting on his hands and drawing back his axe as if to start cutting the tree.*] He's your meat if you can find him.

AASE. Yes, yes. [*She reaches for her basket of clothes, then is struck by a thought. She whirls angrily on* PEER.] Oh, my God, what lies, what lies! [*She bows half over, her feet wide, her hands on her knees, staring at him.*] I remember it now—plain as day. Twenty years ago I heard that tale—before your father come a-courting me.

PEER. [*Cheerfully.*] Things like that can happen twice.

AASE. Sometimes I wish I was dead. You frustrate the life out of me! [*Piteously.*] Beggings and tears don't make a bit of impression on you. You're a lost soul, Peer, lost and undone. That's what you are. The new preacher says so.

PEER. [*Smiles suddenly and sunnily at her. Placatingly.*] Come on now, you fussy old mother.

[*He reaches out with one hand and takes her caressingly by the shoulder. She jerks away from him.*]

AASE. Lies! Lies! Tales! Tales! [*Storming.*] And me a poor, helpless widow! And the farm! The fences falling down! The fields all growing up in briers and brambles. And everything mortgaged, lock, stock, and barrel.

PEER. [*Buoyantly.*] Oh, shut up that old woman's talk.

AASE. [*Wiping her eyes with her apron.*] Old woman's talk! And look at you, big and strong and muscled up— able to support me in my weakness and old age—if you would. But you won't. You won't. [*Ragingly.*] Phooey, phooey! [*She spits at him and he jumps out of the way.*] You deadbeat! You'll bring me down to the grave before my time.

PEER. There you go quarrelling again. I give you my word, Mother— [*He walks about holding his axe. Suddenly he turns on her.*] Some of these days I will make you proud of me. You just wait and see. The whole village someday will look up to you. Just wait till I have done something—something really great. [*He clenches his free fist and shoots it up in a strong affirmation of confidence and will.*] And I'll do it yet.

AASE. [*Snorting in mockery.*] "Someday, someday." You've already paved a street in hell with your lies and promises. [*She turns sharply and weepingly back to work.*]

PEER. Give me time.

AASE. Give you time, and you already a grown man. [*Beating the clothes again.*] You could have made something of yourself, Peer. [*This is an old story to him, and he shrugs his shoulders.*] But no—day in, day out, you've got to loaf and loll around—dreaming and spinning your crazy stories. [*She gestures beyond the fence to the valley below.*] That Hegstadt girl down there was sweet on you. Ingrid loved you, Peer, she did.

PEER. Ingrid. [*Lightly, as he stares up in the trees again.*] Well, suppose she did.

AASE. She still loves you. And Peer, darling, she's a mighty rich girl. [*She wipes her eyes again.*] She's a fine girl, too. Oh, if only you had behaved yourself—you'd be married to her right this minute. [*Her sorrows overflowing again as she rages.*] Look at you, dirty and stinking—walking in rotten rags! A fine bridegroom you'd be for any woman.

PEER. [*A thought suddenly striking him.*] Come on, then, we'll go a-courting Ingrid again.

AASE. [*Scathingly.*] You?

PEER. Yes, me.

AASE. Your time's gone by. Your luck's run out.

PEER. [*Complacently.*] Peer's luck never runs out—with the girls.

AASE. [*Chuckles grimly.*] While you were off in the mountains riding that reindeer through the air, Mads Moen won the girl.

PEER. [*Astounded.*] What, that scarecrow? Mads Moen!

AASE. Yes, Mads Moen! She's taking him for her husband this very day.

[*She gazes over at* PEER *with accusing, red-rimmed eyes. The news socks him hard. His pride is hurt. He turns restlessly about, thinking. A decision comes to him. He laughs.*]

PEER. Hey there, Mother. [*Dropping the axe, he is over to her with a bound and sweeps her up in his arms.*]

AASE. [*Terrified.*] Turn me loose.

[*She kicks and scratches at him, but he pitches her up across his shoulder like a sack of grain.*]

PEER. [*Laughing.*] We'll go down to the wedding together. [*He starts trotting about the scene, jostling her up and down.*]

AASE. [*Squealing.*] Peer! Peer!

PEER. [*Galloping.*] Now you're riding that buck on Gendin Ridge. [*Stampeding about.*] How do you like it? [AASE *shrieks.* PEER *slows down.*] Give the buck a nice kiss then, huh?

AASE. [*Striking him on the ear.*] That's the kiss I'll give you.

PEER. [*Standing still.*] You can still put in a good word for me with Ingrid.

AASE. [*Fiercely.*] I'll put in a good word about your devil's mommicking and the way you treat your poor old mother. That's the good word I'll tell her.

PEER. [*Mockingly scandalized.*] Be ashamed.

AASE. [*Trying to kick loose in her fury.*] And I'll tell them all of your sins and doings—till old man Hegstadt sicks his dogs on you. [*She kicks loose from* PEER, *then puts herself to rights. Weeping, she goes over and grabs up her basket of wet clothes, turning back the way she came. As she passes by* PEER, *she looks out at him with flaming face—a face filled with mortification, anger, and yet unwilling love.*] You—you louse! [*She spits at him again and goes back the way she came.*]

PEER. [*Calling after her, teasingly.*] What a way for a mother to talk to her only son! [AASE *goes out at the left rear toward her little house.* PEER *stands looking after her, his lips stuck out in an impish whistle. He turns and looks over the fence toward the valley below. His restlessness has increased.*] It's not far down to Hegstadt's. I could get there in a jiffy. I bet Ingrid's sitting down there now—thinking of me—lonely— [*He picks up his axe, goes across to the fence, puts one leg over it, and then stops.*] Oh, the devil—why should I want to go down there? [*He shades his eyes against the light in the valley as he stares off. Then he swings his leg back and comes away from the fence. He stands thinking.*] If a fellow had a good slug of liquor—to warm him up—he wouldn't care if they'd laugh at him or not. [*He stares longingly off, then sits down on the ground and leans back against the fence, his axe lying across his lap. He stretches out his clenched fists in a yawn.*

Several people, dressed in their Sunday garb, come along the road beyond the fence. They are on their way to the wedding in the valley below. They see PEER *lying on the ground.*]

AN ELDERLY MAN. Peer Gynt's down drunk again. [*Drawing himself up.*] Well, his father was a drunkard before him.

AN ELDERLY WOMAN. Like father, like son. No wonder his mother's crazy.

[*The others nod their comment and move on out at the left rear beyond the fence.* PEER *sits suddenly up.*]

PEER. [*Almost snarling.*] Talk—talk! Bite with your sharp tongues! Who cares! [*He lays himself back again, his hands under his head, staring up into the sky. The pain and sultry grief pass out of his face. His voice rises in a monologue, growing in fervency. The scene begins to fill again with the feeling of his mood—shadowing off into a darkening around him, but with a radiance filling the unseen sky above and silvering down on his face.*] I bet it's a million miles to that sky. Far, far. And there's a cloud up there, a teeny cloud and the wind blows it closer. It's got a shape to it—um—like a horse. [*His voice intense.*] And it's saddled and bridled, and a man riding. And behind an old woman on a broomstick. [*He laughs softly to himself.*] That's Mother. She's running after me, quarrelling and screaming. [*Calling in a high, faraway voice.*] "You filthy pig! Hey there, Peer, Peer!" [*He is silent. His words are heard echoing across the valley, mocking and diminishing. For a moment he lies listening.*] Let her scream. For that's me riding on that horse, me riding there. Peer Gynt, and a multitude of folks are riding behind. That's my servants. And look at my horse with its silver mane all r'ared up and his four gold horseshoes gleaming. Yay-ee, we go galloping in the sun! [*Excitedly.*] Like a great king riding in the sky! [*He sits sharply up.*] Peer Gynt on the highway of

heaven. [*Staring up and off.*] And look there at the people waiting—a nation of people waiting. It's the Crown
Prince of England, and the beautiful women of England. [*Loudly.*] Greetings, sir. And for you lovely ladies
jewels and a kiss for each pair of ruby red lips. [SOLVEIG
*and her father, a grave Lutheran minister, come in along
the road on their way to the wedding. With them walks*
ASLAK, *the blacksmith, his tall form looming behind
them.* SOLVEIG *is a demure and beautiful young girl. Her
hair hangs down her back like a cascade of gold, and she
carries a white prayer book in her hand.* PEER *continues
his monologue.*] They bow low before me. The King of
England himself steps down from his throne to greet me.
"King Peer," he says—

ASLAK. [*Has spied* PEER *through the fence. He leans
far over now and glares at* PEER. *Blurting out with
huge mockery.*] Peer Gynt, you drunken swine.

PEER. [*Looks around and then springs to his feet, grabbing up his axe, his eyes blazing. Angrily.*] Oh, it's
Aslak, the blacksmith! [*Scornfully.*] What do you want?

ASLAK. [*Laughing.*] We haven't seen you lately, Peer.
Where have you been?

[SOLVEIG'S *parents march on, gesturing her to follow
after, but the blacksmith reaches out and takes her arm,
stopping her.*]

PEER. [*Sulkily, his eyes fastened on* SOLVEIG.] None of
your business.

ASLAK. [*Jovially.*] Solveig, this is Peer Gynt. A mighty
man he is. I whipped him recently in a wrastling match.

[SOLVEIG *glances out at* PEER *and then drops her eyes.*]

PEER. [*Gazing at* SOLVEIG.] That's a lie. I bloodied your nose all right.

ASLAK. [*Winks at* SOLVEIG.] Listen at him. And they say he has dirty doings with witches and trolls in the hills.

PEER. [*Hotly.*] That's another lie.

ASLAK. [*Bows in mock apology.*] Slander and gossip no doubt. And everything is lies. But where have you been lately, Peer?

PEER. [*Simply.*] I have been off doing some big things, Aslak.

ASLAK. [*Winks again at* SOLVEIG.] Oh, you have? Tell Solveig. She's just moved here. Her father's the new minister.

PEER. [*Earnestly, to* SOLVEIG.] That I have. You believe me, don't you?

ASLAK. Sure, we believe you.

PEER. [*Loudly.*] Shut up.

ASLAK. [*Chuckling.*] Same old temper, hot as fire. Come on, Solveig. [*He starts escorting* SOLVEIG *away, then calls back.*] We're going to Ingrid's wedding. Coming?

PEER. [*Roughly.*] I might and I might not.

ASLAK. Maybe you're not invited.

PEER. [*Hotly.*] I'm invited, all right.

ASLAK. Hah-hah-hah.

PEER. You black devil. [*He is about to spring over the fence and come at the blacksmith.*]

ASLAK. [*Stepping back a bit.*] Whee-ew. Look at him
spit flames. [*Jeeringly.*] I'll tell the bride Peer Gynt sends
greetings.

PEER. I'll bring my own greetings.

[ASLAK *starts away.* SOLVEIG *stands where she is.* PEER
*comes along the fence slowly toward her. She lowers her
eyes, blushing. He would speak to her. The blacksmith
turns impatiently back. Crooking his arm and offering it
to* SOLVEIG, *he moves her firmly away.* PEER *stares after
her.*

*A burst of music comes in on the air from the right
rear—a folk dance tune played by a few country musicians.* PEER *continues to gaze after* SOLVEIG. *Abstractedly he begins clapping his hands together in rhythm to
the coming music. His feet as if feeling the tune move
restlessly and dancingly. The scene brightens again.
Along the road at the back enter a number of people on
their way to the wedding. A* YOUNG MOUNTAIN GIRL *in
folk costume is stepping in front as she plays her flute.
With her is a stringy* YELLOW-HAIRED YOUTH *plucking
a lute in accompaniment, his long angular legs in their
tight-fitting britches jerking and jumping joyously as
he plays. Behind them comes the bridegroom,* MADS
MOEN, *a slight young fellow as straight as a string and
with a pale face. His hair is plastered down and he carries his hat in his hands. A huge flower blooms in his
buttonhole. Behind him is a little gnomish,* MIDDLE-AGED
FELLOW *with a bass drum. He is beating it in accompaniment to the music. They all keep their faces set stonily
and straight ahead of them, not noticing* PEER *as they
continue on down the road.*

Lured on by the music, PEER *springs over the fence. He*

looks up the road and then down it. He runs along the fence behind the rock and an instant later emerges with a handful of huge wildflowers. He grabs up his axe by the fence and with it and the flowers goes gaily and brag-gingly on after the music which is now weakening in the distance.

The light begins to die out on the stage. At this instant a part of the "rocky" pile starts to move, and we see the figure of a sleeper or watcher there emerge. It is the BUTTONMOLDER. *He strolls off in the direction taken by* PEER. *The music continues as the scene changes.*]

PART ONE

Scene II

The farmyard at Hegstadt. The light has changed more to the color of lowland, of leafery and greenery. A tree has appeared at the back splashing its shadows coolingly on the ground. At the right rear, the corner of the farmhouse is now seen with steps leading into it.

The THREE MUSICIANS *come marching in from the left front, lively and joyous. They are playing as they come. Behind them a medley of people, young, middle-aged and old, come in laughing and chattering—vocables shrill and soaring of the girls and the women, the masculine and earth-proud bass of the young and middle-aged men, and the piping of the elderly ones. A table loaded with viands is pushed in by some of the young people as they enter. The movements of all the people are emphatic and rhythmic as in a dance. And now as the music changes they are actually dancing. A line of girls is on the right and the young men on the left. They meet in the center, take partners and go sailing happily about.*

The older guests collect around the table in the rear—in their pantomime simulating eating and drinking.

The dance in the foreground builds toward its climax of pleasure. The feeling created in it affects even the older ones at the rear. Their bodies move and stir rhythmically. The LITTLE ELDERLY MAN *with his bass drum flails away on it and begins walking up and down across the scene all r'ared back, in time to the music. The* MASTER COOK *comes to the door of the little house and looks out beamingly. He steps swiftly down to the table and hands out drink in mugs.*

And now highlighted in the center are ASLAK, *the smith, and his partner* SOLVEIG. *He showers his tenderness and great strength protectingly and lovingly upon her and around her. But she is reserved and somewhat unresponsive.*

MADS MOEN, *the bridegroom, comes in at the right rear. He glances timidly behind him. The* MASTER COOK *waves his dipper in the air.*

COOK. Hooray for Mads Moen!

VOICES. Hooray for the bridegroom!

[MADS MOEN *lifts his hand in shy greeting, his face filled with stifling selfconsciousness. Some of the* DRINKERS *move up around him and lift their mugs clinkingly above his head.*]

DRINKERS. Lucky Mads Moen.

A WOMAN'S VOICE. [*High and a little satirical.*] But what about the bride?

ANOTHER WOMAN'S VOICE. Where's the bride?

VOICES. Ingrid—where is Ingrid?

COOK. [*Gaily.*] She'll be coming in all her finery and glory. Get ready, Mads Moen, get ready.

A BOY. [*To* MADS.] Drink, fellow, drink.

COOK. Let the jug go round, people. Drink and be merry.

A BOY. Music—let the music roll.

A GIRL. [*Shrilly.*] Saw on the strings.

[ASLAK *begins to do his stuff with* SOLVEIG. *The attention passes from the bridegroom. The young people now ring around the smith and his beauteous partner.* ASLAK *holds* SOLVEIG'S *hand aloft and passes around her, then in front of her and back, as if she were a maypole, his heavy-booted feet jiggling and squirming furiously.*]

A GIRL. [*Admiringly.*] He's got limber legs, all right.

ANOTHER GIRL. I've seen him kick clean to the ceiling.

[ASLAK *cuts a few terrific steps, recovers himself and stands bowing to the applause breaking around him. The* DANCERS *move thirstily toward the table in the rear.* MADS MOEN *and his father are now left standing downstage. His father is a stout burgher type of man and is enjoying his mug of drink.*]

MADS. [*Piteously.*] She won't, Father!

MOEN. [OLD MOEN *lowers his mug and looks sharply at his timid son.*] She won't—what?

MADS. Ingrid won't speak to me. She's gone and locked herself in the house. [*He gestures off to the right rear.*]

MOEN. [*Angrily.*] Break down the door!

MADS. Ooh—I—I don't know how—I can't, Father.

MOEN. [*Explosively.*] You fool!

[*He turns toward the table at the rear for a refill of his mug.* MADS *stands alone, forlorn and uncertain. He turns and goes slowly back the way he came.*

PEER GYNT *shows up at the right front carrying his axe by the helve in one hand and his bunch of flowers in the other. He stands looking in on the scene. His unkempt hair, poor shirt and tattered trousers contrast sharply with the holiday folk dress of the wedding guests and dancers. A tittering and whispering begin among the boys and girls.* PEER *stands there, somewhat hesitant and shamefaced. Some of the* DRINKERS *lower their mugs from their lips and glance out at* PEER. *He takes a tentative step forward and smiles disarmingly. The* LONG, GANGLING BOY *who plays the fiddle points at him with his bow.*]

FIDDLER. [*In a high, satirical call.*] Peer Gynt has come!

VOICES. Peer Gynt! Peer Gynt!

BOY. There'll be plenty of doings now.

ASLAK [*Steps quickly out and stares at* PEER. *To the* COOK.] Who asked *him?*

COOK. [*Shrugging.*] Nobody.

[*The* YOUNG GIRLS *with the exception of* SOLVEIG, *prompted by their curiosity, now move a little bit toward* PEER. ASLAK *puts out a big and commanding hand to stop them.*]

ASLAK. [*Sternly, to the girls.*] Pay no attention to him. Don't notice him.

A DARKEYED GIRL. [*Staring at* PEER *with bold eyes.*]
We'll act like we don't even see him.

[*She smiles at* PEER, *showing her white teeth. As if encouraged,* PEER *comes quickly forward.*]

PEER. [*Boldly.*] Who is the liveliest girl in the ring?

DARKEYED GIRL. [*Draws quickly back from him.*] Not
me.

ANOTHER GIRL. [*In the same manner.*] And not me.

A THIRD GIRL. And me neither.

PEER. [*To the fourth, a homely one.*] Well then, how
about you—[*Grimacing.*]—before a better one turns
up? [*He laughs brutally.*]

HOMELY GIRL. [*Turning her back on him.*] I am just going home.

PEER. [*Alarmed.*] Home? It's early. You all can't be
leaving now.

HOMELY GIRL. [*Stoutly and coldly.*] I've got no time
for the likes of you.

[*The people laugh.*]

PEER. [*Insolently, to a fifth girl.*] All right, you, come
on.

FIFTH GIRL. I am not that bad off for a man.

[*She moves over and takes the arm of a* MIDDLE-AGED
FELLOW *with squinting eye and a heavy moustache. The
people laugh.*]

ASLAK. [*Jeering at* PEER.] She likes an old fellow better.

COOK. [*Singing out.*] Poor Peer Gynt. He can't find a girl.

[PEER *is angered. He half draws back his axe as if to protect himself against the hurt of their tirade. Then he glances hiddenly and shyly toward the group as if courting their favor, but they all look at him silently. He turns about the yard. Cold eyes greet him everywhere.*]

PEER. [*Snarling suddenly to himself.*] Look at their smiles—sharp as nails. [*Wiping his sleeve across his mouth.*] And their eyes, too, digging in your flesh like fishhooks. [*Raging inwardly.*] If I had my butcher knife I'd cut their hearts out.

[*He fastens his eyes on* SOLVEIG. *He shudders and glides along the ground toward her, holding the flowers out. As she reaches to take them,* ASLAK *grabs them away and tosses them far behind him. Others grab them up, toss them about like a plaything between them, and finally out of the scene.* SOLVEIG *follows the bouncing bouquet with her eyes.* PEER *blinks and looks at* ASLAK, *hate hardening within him. The people laugh again.* PEER *looks at* SOLVEIG, *now as if for help. He turns his back on the others, gazing only at her. His face softens. He bows slightly to* SOLVEIG'S *father, the* MINISTER.]

PEER. [*Elegantly, courteously.*] May I dance with your daughter, sir?

MINISTER. [*Uncertainly.*] But first we must pay our respects to the host.

[*He turns back toward the house with* SOLVEIG *and her* MOTHER. *Everybody now gathers around the table.* PEER *stands left behind. The* COOK *lifts his dipper high and calls over to him.*]

COOK. Since you've come anyhow, Peer, you might as well drink with us.

PEER. I am not thirsty. I've come to do some dancing. [*He gazes longingly after* SOLVEIG *over at the house. The light, as if following the bent of his imagination, illuminates her more brightly than the others, who are somewhat shadowed down.* PEER'S *poetic soul begins to feel enraptured. He talks to himself.*] I have never seen a girl like her before. With her little shoes and her white apron and her eyes looking down all modest-like. And she still carries her prayer book wrapped in a cloth. And her hair like gold!

[*He shakes his head as if touched with wonder, and then suddenly he dashes over toward* SOLVEIG *to seize her and pull her spasmodically into a dance. But* ASLAK *steps swiftly in front of him and pushes him back.* PEER *stops and stands looking at the formidable smith.*]

A BOY. [*As* PEER *stands still.*] Peer's afraid of the blacksmith.

ANOTHER BOY. [*Singingly.*] Peer's afraid of Aslak.

PEER. Get out of my way.

[*He flings his axe aside and balls up his fists ready to fight. The people grow tense.* SOLVEIG *pushes her way quickly through the crowd and comes up to* PEER.]

SOLVEIG. [*Softly.*] You wanted to dance with me? [PEER *nods shyly. The boy with the fiddle starts the music up again.* ASLAK *moves forward to snatch the two apart. But* PEER, *putting his arm around* SOLVEIG'S *waist, swirls her away out of his reach. Several of the* DRINKERS, *now feeling merry enough for fair play, push* ASLAK back. PEER *lives only for the moment of this joy. The light accommodates him to his wish and emphasizes him and* SOLVEIG *while the other people in the scene are dimmed down. As the dance progresses,* SOLVEIG *shows she is somewhat bothered by* PEER'S *vehement manner. Presently.*] Just for a little while, Mother said.

PEER. [*Mockingly.*] Mother said—Mother said. Are you still a baby?

SOLVEIG. [*A little stiffly.*] I'm grown up. I was confirmed last spring.

[*He tries to kiss her. She breaks angrily loose from him. He follows her contritely toward the group at the back.*]

PEER. Solveig—

[MADS MOEN *comes running in and tugs at his mother's apron. She turns him around into the scene downstage as the eating and merrymaking recede toward the rear.*]

MADS. Mother, Ingrid won't—

MRS. MOEN. Won't what?

MADS. Won't, Mother.

MRS. MOEN. What?

MADS. Open the door for me.

[MRS. MOEN *throws up her hands in irritation and scorn.*]

MOEN. [*Breaking in angrily.*] You calf! You ought to be tied in a stall.

[*He pushes his mug into* MADS' *hand and forces him to take a drink.* SOLVEIG *is now seen escaping* PEER'S *atten-*

tion. She moves over to her father and takes his arm for protection.]

A MAN. Solveig's afraid of you, Peer.

ANOTHER MAN. She better be. He'll dirty you, Solveig.

[*The people laugh again.*]

COOK. [*Holding a dipper full of drink out toward* PEER.] A little hot stuff, Peer.

[PEER *glances about, hesitates, then grabs up a mug and holds it for the* COOK *to fill. He drains it empty without lowering it from his lips and holds it for a refill. He drinks that down, then throws the mug behind him and glares determinedly about him. He makes a move toward one of the girls.*]

GIRL. [*Hurriedly to a companion.*] Come on, let's go.

PEER. [*Gazes at the girls now. His smile is malevolent and crooked. Loudly.*] You girls are all afraid of me.

A BOY. [*Cackling.*] Everybody's afraid of you.

A WOMAN'S VOICE. [*Scornfully.*] Such a lover.

A MAN'S VOICE. [*Likewise.*] Such a great fighter.

A GIRL'S VOICE. Such a trickster! He can do tricks.

VOICES. Tricks! Tricks!

[*The young people whisper among themselves and then suddenly make a swooshing charge at* PEER *and encircle him. The music stops.*]

THE DARKEYED GIRL. Show us a conjure trick, Peer.

VOICES. Yes, yes.

OTHER VOICES. He knows witchcraft.

PEER. [*Beginning to be warmed and excited by the liquor. He nods "yes" and speaks up strongly. Ominously.*] I might conjure up the devil.

A MAN. [*Laughing.*] Grandma could do that easy enough.

PEER. I can do things nobody else can. Once I conjured the devil into a wormhole in a walnut.

[*Several people nod their heads agreeably.*]

PEOPLE. [*Laughing.*] We believe you if you say so, Peer.

PEER. [*More loudly.*] I stuffed the hole with a splinter. Hey, you shoulda heard him buzz and tremble. "Please, Mr. Peer," he said, "I'll give you a piece of new money— gold—gold I'll give you if you'll let me out"—gold like Solveig's shining hair.

A GIRL. [*In mock excitement.*] Now, think of that.

PEER. Yessir, he buzzed just like a great big bumblebee.

ANOTHER GIRL. [*Shrilly.*] Have you still got him in that walnut, Peer?

PEER. I would have but for Aslak here. [*Indicating the still angry blacksmith.*] You know what a long nose he's got for other people's business. [ASLAK *throws up his hands in angry dismissal.*] "What you got there?" he says to me. "I got the devil all shut up," I says. "Let me at him and I'll bust him out," he says. So I put the walnut on his anvil and he hauled back with a sledgehammer— [*He suddenly points a dirty and powerful finger at the blacksmith.*] He pulled back his sledgehammer to smash the devil.

A VOICE. Did he?

ANOTHER VOICE. Did he smash him to pieces?

PEER. [*Enjoying himself.*] "Watch out, Aslak," I said,
"he's mighty tough. That old imp, he's mighty tough."
But Aslak's a man. And he brung his hammer down,
hard as life would let him. [*He screws up his face again.*]

ASLAK. [*Hissing.*] Listen at the fool! Listen.

PEER. But the devil took care of himself, all right. Wham
went the hammer! Then a flash of flame like a firecracker.
Straight through the roof the devil split. And a shower
of burning shingles fell all over the place. [*He leaps high
in the air and several of the girls jump back with little
screams.*]

VOICES. And the blacksmith—what happened to him?

PEER. [*Dramatically.*] He got his hands all roasted and
burnt for his trouble—and his hammer flew up in the
sky and fell beyond Gendin Ridge. [*Imitating the whistle of a falling shell and then snapping his fingers.*]
That's why Aslak's been afraid of me ever since—me
and the devil.

[*He thumbs his nose at* ASLAK. *The people laugh in high
good spirits, and the* LITTLE MAN *taps softly on his bass
drum, its hollow sound going dum, dum in the scene.*]

VOICES. That's a good lie.

OTHER VOICES. Almost one of his best.

PEER. [*Angrily.*] You think I make up everything? Do
you?

A MAN. Oh no, you don't make it up. [*To those about*

him.] I heard that same story from my old grand-
daddy.

PEER. [*Fiercely.*] It happened to me.

A MAN. [*Smiling.*] So has everything else.

[*The* DARKEYED GIRL *goes by* PEER *and laughs teasingly and mockingly in his face. He grabs her by the arm
and pours his hot words full at her.*]

PEER. Hey, I can ride through the air! I can, I tell you.
[*The people laugh again.*] I've done it. Yes, I have.

A BOY. [*Running out at* PEER *and flapping his arms like
a bird.*] Ride through the air now, Peer Gynt.

PEER. And I can turn into a troll, too—when I want to.

OTHER VOICES. Let's see you do it, Peer.

STILL OTHER VOICES. [*Ad lib.*] Yes, Peer, yes. Be a troll
for us.

PEER. [*Glaring about him.*] Laugh, laugh. But someday I'll ride over you all. And you'll all be bowing down
before me.

OLDER MAN. [*Nodding in the air, confirmingly.*] Now
he's really crazy.

ANOTHER MAN. A fool.

A THIRD MAN. Braggart.

A FOURTH MAN. Liar.

PEER. [*Balling up his fists again and raging around in
front of them.*] Wait and see. You just wait.

[*The crowd is now tired of him. The people turn back*

toward the table, ignoring him. Now PEER *stands forlorn as ever the bridegroom was.* MADS MOEN *comes up to him.*]

MADS. [*Timidly.*] Is it true, Peer?

PEER. [*Abruptly.*] Of course it is, Mads. I'm a really terrible fellow.

MADS. [*Shakes his head in wonder.*] And you've got a magic cape, the way you say.

PEER. [*Abstractedly, as he watches* SOLVEIG.] A magic hat, you mean. Yes, I've got that, Mads. And when I put it on you can't see me—I raise such a dust.

[SOLVEIG *starts by the table.* PEER *catches her wrist.*]

SOLVEIG. Let me go. [*Tearfully.*] You're so wild.

PEER. Aye, like the reindeer buck in the summertime.

SOLVEIG. [*Pulling back.*] You've been drinking.

[*She jerks loose from him again and hurries around at the left of the table.* MADS *pushes at* PEER *with his elbow.*]

MADS. Can you help me get to Ingrid?

PEER. [*Absentmindedly.*] Ingrid—where is she?

MADS. Shut up in the house. Oh, you must help me, Peer.

PEER. [*Disgustedly.*] You'll have to handle her yourself. [*A thought shoots up in him. He speaks softly and sharply.*] Ingrid you say. [MADS *gestures eagerly off toward the house.* PEER *grabs his arm.* MADS *leads the way off toward the right rear.* PEER *stops close to* SOLVEIG. *He speaks up accusingly.*] You're afraid of me.

SOLVEIG. [*As if ashamed.*] That's not true.

PEER. I know I'm a little drunk, but that's because you hurt me. [*He reaches out to her.*] Let's finish our dance. [SOLVEIG *shakes her head. His eyes bore into hers.*] I can turn myself into a troll. You heard me say so. [*She smiles slightly in disbelief, though her face is still hurt.*] Better look out. I'll stand by your bed tonight at twelve o'clock. [*The smile passes from her face and she looks at him sorrowfully and pityingly.*] And when you hear something hiss and spitting in the dark, you needn't think it's the cat. [*He goes on brutally.*] It'll be me. I might drain your blood in a cup. [*The people are now watching* PEER *again, gesturing with their food-filled hands and nodding their heads as much as to say, "There's that fool telling Solveig his big lies."*] I can turn myself into a werewolf at night too. [*He pushes up close to* SOLVEIG *as she backs away from him. He barks his words out.*] I'll bite you—bite you all over your legs and back. [*His voice suddenly changes and he speaks softly and beggingly to her.*] Dance with me, Solveig.

SOLVEIG. [*Frightened and gazing at him drearily.*] Why do you behave so—so ugly! [*She pushes quickly from him and disappears into the crowd at the rear.*]

MADS. [*Pulling at* PEER'S *sleeve.*] I'll give you a good ox if you'll help me get Ingrid. Just for yourself a good work ox.

PEER. [*Snarling.*] Come on.

[*He starts striding across the scene toward the right rear. The blacksmith flings the people away from him and accosts* PEER, *pulling off his jacket.*]

COOK. [*Calling out.*] No fighting now!

ASLAK. We'll see who's a liar and a coward. I'll rub his face in the dirt, so help me!

[*Some of the people pull at the blacksmith but others egg him on.*]

VOICE. Yes, let them fight.

ANOTHER VOICE. Run Peer Gynt out of here.

STILL ANOTHER VOICE. Yea, kick him out, Aslak.

ASLAK. [*Throws his jacket to one side.*] This time I'll break his neck.

[*He draws back his fist. But* PEER *suddenly snaps his fingers in his face, laughs, grabs up his axe, and runs off around the house after* MADS. ASLAK *fumbles about him for his jacket to run after him. The people send their jeers after the cowardly* PEER. AASE *comes in with a stick in her hand. She peers about her with her red-rimmed eyes.*]

AASE. Is that son of mine here? Just let me get my hands on him.

[ASLAK *shakes out his jacket disgustedly and begins putting it on.*]

A VOICE. Aslak's going to beat him to pieces.

ASLAK. I'll choke his guts out. [*He spits on his hands and goes through the quick pantomime of throttling* PEER *in the air before him.*]

AASE. [*Whirling on him.*] Hurt my Peer! Oh, no you won't! [*She slaps her flat chest defiantly.*] Old Aase still has teeth and claws to defend him. Where is he? [*She calls loudly over the scene.*] Peer!

[*A girl's sudden scream in the distance answers her. The people turn in the direction of the cry.* MADS MOEN *comes running in, terrified.*]

MADS. Father, Father—Mother, Mother!

MOEN. What's happened?

MADS. Peer Gynt— [*He chokes up and gestures help- lessly behind him.*]

AASE. What's happened to my boy! [*She springs over to the right rear and looks off. Now she lets out a scream in her turn and points with her stick.*]

MOEN. [*Yelling.*] Look up the height there!

VOICES. With the bride!

OTHER VOICES. He's got Ingrid in his arms!

AASE. [*Moaning.*] The brute!

ASLAK. [*Thunderstruck.*] He's climbing up that steep cliff with her—God help me—like a goat!

MADS. [*Weeping.*] He's carrying her off, Mother. Like a pig in his arms he's carrying her.

INGRID'S MOTHER. Ingrid! Ingrid!

AASE. [*Shaking her fist toward the unseen and fleeing* PEER.] May God make you fall! [*Screaming again in fear.*] Watch out, Peer!

INGRID'S FATHER. [*Stands in front of everybody, bare- headed and white with anger.*] I'll have his life for steal- ing my daughter!

AASE. You shan't harm him! I won't let you.

INGRID'S FATHER. Come on!

[*He gestures to the young men about him, and they set out running off at the right in pursuit of the fleeing* PEER, *hallooing as they go.* AASE *raises her stick and goes swiftly after them to protect* PEER. *A murmur of fear runs among the young people and they gaze about them. The sky darkens, and a wind begins blowing through the scene, shaking the leaves of the trees.*

The scene begins to fade. And now the LITTLE MAN *starts his drum beat, monotonous and pursuing, as if accompanying the footfalls of the posse. He hurries out of the scene, beating rhythmically as he goes. The shouting and the tumult fade, and so does the sound of the drum. They continue in the distance as the light dies out.*]

PART ONE

Scene III

The drum has continued beating and the shoutings and halloos far away. The light comes up again revealing a cleared space high in the mountains. It is near dawn, and the grey misty light of morning fills the void at the back. A foot-trail crosses the foreground, and in the middle background we see the upjutting treeless rocks stabbing across the wide vista which reaches toward the distant foggy snow-clad peaks.

PEER GYNT comes moving along the path, carrying his axe in his hand, and INGRID HEGSTADT is trying to pull him back. She is a young girl of seventeen or eighteen. Normally spirited and very pretty, she is now woebegone and pale in her pitiful, dilapidated bridal clothes.

PEER. [*Snapping at her.*] Get away from me, will you?

INGRID. Where'll I go? [*Boohooing.*] Where—after what you've done to me?

PEER. I don't care where. [*Brutally.*] Just so you get out of my sight.

INGRID. [*Wringing her hands.*] You deceived me—betrayed me.

36

PEER. Go on. Go on. Leave me alone.

INGRID. Oh, oh!

PEER. [*Striking the butt of his axe on the ground with a thud.*] The devil take you—take all women, I say. [*Suddenly thoughtful, then adding softly.*] Except one.

INGRID. Except one? Who?

PEER. Not you.

INGRID. [*Piteously.*] Dear, sweet Peer.

PEER. [*Yelling.*] Shut up! [*Turning sharply on her.*] Do I see a prayer book in your hand? No. And what about your hair? Is it a shower of gold down your back? No. And where is your white apron? And were you confirmed in the church? Do you hold to your mother's skirt like an innocent child? "Mother said. Mother said." [INGRID *backs away from his vehemence. He is shouting.*] Do you?

INGRID. No, but—

PEER. Do you look at a man modestly? No, you don't. Can you refuse me—when I ask you to give? Can you? No. You give everything willingly. I don't even have to ask you.

INGRID. Mercy, he's crazy.

PEER. [*Bending toward her and staring intently in her face.*] Does a man feel something good and sacred in his heart—when he looks at you? Does he?

INGRID. [*Pleadingly.*] You'd be rich if you married me. You'd be respected in the community, looked up to.

[*Bursting into tears.*] Oh, Peer, you've ruined me, ruined me!

PEER. You were willing enough.

INGRID. Father will kill you for this.

PEER. [*With a sudden loud yell at her.*] To hell with you! [INGRID *turns her head away.*] To hell with all women.

INGRID. [*Scornfully.*] Except one.

PEER. [*Yelling again.*] Yea, except one.

[*He threatens to strike her. She runs away at the left front, weeping bitterly. He glances after her and kicks angrily with his foot and souses his axe blade deep in the ground. The low faint beat of the drum is heard in the distance, mixed with the hallooing voices of the posse. PEER lifts his head and listens. A chuckle comes from the rocks behind him. He starts, then turns frantically about. He looks this way and that for the mocking voice. As if in keeping with his darksome apprehension, the scene gradually deepens with gloom. Now the snow-tipped mountains in the distance are lost in the shadows. A wind whooms in the valley beyond the rocks. A flash of lightning breaks, and then the banging rattle of reverberating thunder. PEER beats his fists together above his waiting axe, prancing about in irresolution. AASE is heard calling in the rising wind.*]

AASE'S VOICE. Peer! Peer!

[*He jerks his axe up and runs off at the right rear. AASE and* SOLVEIG *come in from the left rear.* AASE *holds a lantern before her to light the way.*]

AASE. The powers of evil are abroad this night. The mists, the waters, and the cursed mountains—look at them. The watery elements turmoiling to confuse him and drown him in these bottomless chasms. [*Listening.*] And the people! They are out to kill him. [*She holds her lantern up higher, peering about her.*] But the mercy of God won't let them do it. No. Oh, the scoundrel. Why does he let the devil tempt him so? [*Turning to* SOLVEIG.] I can't believe he's done this evil thing. He was always full of lies and makebelieves about emperors and kings and stolen brides. Talk, talk—romancing, and romancing. Never doing a stroke of work. But it wasn't talk. The evil was in him. [*Far in the distance a halloo is heard from one of the pursuers.* AASE *is terrified.*] Hoo! What a scream. It's a nixie or goblin, Solveig. They're after him.

SOLVEIG. We must help him. [*Frantically.*] We'll go ring the church bells.

AASE. [*Lifting her voice in a high call.*] Peer! Peer!

[*From the mountains far away comes echoing back once more the elfin mocking words of "Peer, Peer."*]

SOLVEIG. [*Pulling at* AASE'S *sleeve.*] Come away. Let's ring the bells.

[SOLVEIG'S father, the MINISTER, *enters quietly with a lantern from the left rear. He is staring along the ground as if tracking* PEER. AASE *begins to weep.*]

AASE. [*Crying out.*] Peer, Peer, my lost lamb.

MINISTER. Yes, lost. That's right. His soul is lost.

AASE. No, no. Our Lord is kind. He will forgive.

MINISTER. [*Sternly.*] Better if you saw him hanged on a gallows.

AASE. No! No!

MINISTER. [*Relentlessly.*] Under the hangman's hands he might repent of his sins—and save his soul from eternal damnation.

AASE. You run me crazy with your talk. We must find him. [*Shaking the lantern palsily back and forth.*] His life is at stake. [*A crash of thunder nearby jars the earth.*] Merciful Jesus—my boy! My boy!

MINISTER. [*Gazing at the ground under the lantern light.*] Here are the tracks of a man's foot. [*He moves forward.*]

AASE. [*Joyously to* SOLVEIG *as they move off.*] We will find him, Solveig.

SOLVEIG. [*To* AASE *as they go.*] Tell me a little more.

AASE. [*Wiping her eyes.*] About my son?

SOLVEIG. Yes—everything.

AASE. [*Smiles and tosses her head.*] Everything? You'd soon become tired.

SOLVEIG. You'd become tired of talking before I did of hearing.

[*Again from the distance comes the sound of a high halloo.*]

AASE. Hurry.

SOLVEIG. [*Again frantically.*] We must go ring the church bells, to protect him.

AASE. Yes, yes.

[*They turn and hurry swiftly out at the left rear the way they entered. The* MINISTER *looks about him and then moves on out at the right front, hunting for* PEER. *The drum is heard again and a few scattered halloos in the distance. The wind surges up with its musical, almost human plaintiveness and sinks again. Once more the lightning flashes across the void, glimmering through the milky fog, and the rumble of thunder follows.* PEER *comes running in at the right rear. He is panting and tired. His hair is glistening with the congealed drops of the wet night. He looks this way and that.*]

PEER. [*Grimly.*] The whole neighborhood's after me— armed with rifles and clubs! The mob. [*Chuckling.*] Now it's spread far and wide that Peer Gynt, the desperado, is loose in the hills. [*Jubilation breaking in his voice.*] This is something different—from fighting that fool blacksmith. [*Slapping himself.*] This is the real thing. The heart beats in you. The blood jumps—excitement, life. Break, overturn, fight against the rapids. Strike. Yank the fir tree up by the roots.

[*He hits about him with his axe and leaps into the air. A gust of feminine laughter breaks from the rocks beyond.* PEER *springs around. As if activated out of the rocks themselves,* THREE HERD GIRLS *scamper into the scene. They are sassy and sexy, costumed and made up to fit their young, thoughtless woodland lechery. They gallop about the scene and surround* PEER, *screaming and singing in unison.*]

THREE HERD GIRLS.
   Here's a troll, troll, troll

In our arms we feel him roll
Up-a hill and down-a dale
Troll lad, troll lad, never fail!

[*They reach out their arms, and* PEER *stares at them fascinated.*]

PEER. Why do you screech so?

HERD GIRLS. [*Chanting huskily.*]
For trolls! For trolls!

FIRST HERD GIRL. [*Laying her hand on* PEER *strokingly.*]
Treat me easy.

SECOND HERD GIRL. [*Doing likewise.*]
Treat me rough.

[*She wriggles her body up against him.*]

THIRD HERD GIRL. [*Luringly.*]
In the cabin the bed is waiting.

[*They all dance.*]

FIRST HERD GIRL.
Rough is gentle.

SECOND HERD GIRL.
And gentle is rough.

THIRD HERD GIRL.
If we can't get boys
We'll do it with trolls.

THREE HERD GIRLS. [*Together.*]
Boys! Boys!

PEER. Where are the boys?

HERD GIRLS.
> They are gone, gone.

FIRST HERD GIRL.
> Mine called me both his sweetheart and darling.
> Now he is bound to a wrinkled widow.

SECOND HERD GIRL.
> Mine met a gypsy wench north in the mountains.
> Now they are travelling in sin together.

THIRD HERD GIRL.
> Mine took our brat and murdered the bastard.
> His little head grinning is stuck on a pole.

HERD GIRLS. [*Dancing again.*]
> Here's a troll, troll, troll
> In our arms we feel him roll.
> Up-a hill and down-a dale
> Troll lad, troll lad, never fail!

PEER. [*With a leap* PEER *stands among them, dropping his axe behind him. Caught in their manner.*]

> I'm a troll with three heads
> And a three-woman lad.

FIRST HERD GIRL. [*Wildly.*]
> To the cabin! To the cabin!

SECOND HERD GIRL. [*Fondling* PEER.]
> He sparkles and sizzles like red-hot iron.

THIRD HERD GIRL. [*Fondling him likewise.*]
> His baby eyes are black as the mountain pool.

[PEER *begins dancing with them. They start away with him, when from far deep in the mountains there is an-*

other crash of thunder followed by a woman's bass-like voice in a long, deep call.]

WOMAN'S VOICE. Ooh-ah!

[*The* HERD GIRLS *stop instantly as if pierced through. Their phallic excess and feeling fade. They wheel and vanish the way they came.* PEER *turns dizzily about, reaching his hands in front of him as if searching for them. He wags his head back and forth and finally sits down on a rock.*]

PEER. [*Rubbing his forehead.*] It's all make-believe and damned lies, that's what it is. Nothing but dreams and imaginings. [*Muttering.*] Aye, how the fool runs up the steepest cliff—carrying the bride in his arms. [*Mocking a neighbor's cry.*] Hey there, Peer Gynt, Peer Gynt. [*Spitting.*] And lying drunk day and night, chased by hawks and kites, threatened by witches and trolls. Dreams. Dreams. And running around with whoring girls in the woods. Liar! Braggart! Fool! [*He leaps to his feet. A crash of thunder answers his new-found energy.*] I'll get out of here. I'll make a new start. [*The gloom in the foreground fades away with* PEER'S *mood of strong resolve. He turns back toward the rear and stands gazing out and down into the valley.*] I'll get on a ship—go to England. And I'll see the king there—and the women will be— [*Spitting angrily again.*] Hack— women! [*Proudly.*] Peer Gynt, you were born of great folks, though your daddy drank himself in the grave. And someday you're going to be great yourself. [*He whirls about as if to get started instantly toward that greatness, but he bumps into the side of the rock. The rock chuckles and moves. It is the* BUTTONMOLDER. PEER *falls backward horror-struck and almost stunned*

by the impact. The dark figure of the BUTTONMOLDER
looks down at PEER *as he puts out his hand supplicatingly, his head ringing like church bells and queer feelings filling it. The weird bass-like halloo of the woman
is heard close at hand. The* BUTTONMOLDER *chuckles
indulgently and yet sarcastically at* PEER *and looks away
at the right rear. The* GREEN CLAD ONE *appears at the
left rear. She stands radiant in the sudden sunlight,
buxom and procreant—Cybele, Venus, the Whore of
Babylon. Her bronze red hair hangs cascading down behind her, tied with a girl's big green ribbon. Her com-
plexion is a ripened peach, and her lips full and berry-
scarlet. Her seductive green gown is cut low, and her
swelling breasts show in their fecund abundance. She
comes nearer to* PEER. *He gazes up at her, caught by the
invisible force of sex pulling him instantly to her. He
rises hypnotically from the ground.*]

GREENCLAD ONE. Come to me, love, come.

PEER. [*Breathlessly.*] Me? You want me?

GREENCLAD ONE. Yes, you. Only you.

PEER. [*Dreamily, as he reaches out to her.*] Then take
me. You'll see how well I'll behave. You won't have to
spin and weave. I'll provide.

GREENCLAD ONE. And you won't beat me—for I'm a
princess?

PEER. Mercy, no. We sons of kings don't beat our
women.

GREENCLAD ONE. Are you a king's son?

PEER. Of course.

GREENCLAD ONE. I am the Troll King's daughter. In the Ronde Mountain my father has his castle. [PEER *nods.*] So you know my father? He is called King Brose.

PEER. [*As if chanting in antiphonal reply.*] Do you know my mother? She is called Queen Aase. And I'm Prince Peer.

GREENCLAD ONE. And these rags—are they all the clothes you've got?

PEER. You should see my Sunday suit.

GREENCLAD ONE. My weekday dress is of gold and silk.

PEER. [*Gazing at her.*] Looks to me like tow-bagging and straws.

GREENCLAD ONE. Ah, that's a thing you've got to learn. In my father's house black seems white and ugly seems fair.

PEER. And big seems little and dirty clean?

GREENCLAD ONE. [*Nodding.*] Yes. [*She springs forward and falls on* PEER'S *neck.*] Now I see we belong to each other.

PEER. [*Stroking her.*] Like legs to the britches, like hair to the comb.

GREENCLAD ONE. [*Lifts her head and calls in her great voice.*] Bridal steed! Come, my bridal steed!

[*A gigantic pig comes running in at the left front with a bit of rope as a bridle and an old sack tied on him for a saddle.* PEER *gleefully swings himself on the back of the pig and pulls the* GREENCLAD ONE *in front of him.*]

PEER. Away to the king's house! Hurry up, hurry up, my good steed.

GREENCLAD ONE. [*Singing.*]
Oh, yesterday I wandered so lonesome and sad
But today has brought me my golden lad.

[*She shows her pearly teeth in a dazzling smile and hugs the breath out of* PEER. *He gasps drunkenly.*]

PEER. [*Beating the pig as they trot away, his voice a mixture of high spirits and sarcasm.*] You can tell a great man by the horse he rides!

[*The pig grunts loudly in reply. A crash of thunder and lightning, and then the scene fades out.*]

PART ONE

Scene IV

*The Royal Hall of the King of the Trolls. A
gathering of* TROLL COURTIERS, NIXIES *and*
GOBLINS *has assembled. The* KING *is on his
throne with crown and sceptre. The pig on
which* PEER *still sits astride with the now-
drowsy* GREENCLAD ONE *in his arms, is run-
ing around in circles. The* TROLL COURTIERS
*and relatives of the old king are following the
pig and persecuting* PEER. *They are chanting
in a husky and outlandish unison, led now and
then by the* CHAMBERLAIN'S *voice more piercing than the others.*

TROLL COURTIER.
　　Slaughter him!

TROLL COURTIERS. [*Chanting.*]
　　The Christian son has bewitched
　　The Troll King's loveliest maiden.

[*In unison like Negro steel drivers.*]

　　Hanh!

A TROLL BRAT. [*In a high squealing call.*]
　　Let me cut him in the finger.

ANOTHER TROLL BRAT. [*Likewise.*]
　　Let me tear him by the hair.
　　　　　　　　48

A TROLL VIRGIN.
Hu-hi! Let me bite him in the leg.

A TROLL WITCH. [*Stirring the air with a spoon.*]
Let me boil him in a stew.

ANOTHER TROLL WITCH. [*Cutting great slices through the air with a hooked carving knife.*]
Let me roast him on a spit!

[*She whets her knife on her lean hard arm.*]

TROLL KING. [*Intoning in a tremendous voice.*] Let your hot blood cool! [*He waves his* COUNSELORS *closer to him.* PEER *springs off the pig, which runs out of the scene. He nows bears the* GREENCLAD ONE *over toward the throne. He stands holding her saggingly against him as the* KING *confers with his* COUNSELORS, *then speaks.*] Now, let's don't brag. The truth is we've been falling behind in our power in recent times. It's hard to tell what's what any more—what'll turn out good or turn out bad. Still, there's no sense in running good recruits away. Look at him—he's a strongly built fellow.

OLD TROLL. But he's got only one head.

KING. True enough, but my daughter's got only one head herself. [*The* GREENCLAD ONE *straightens up and stands away from* PEER *bowed in front of her father. The* KING *reaches out in a protective motion as he continues.*] Three-headed trolls are going clean out of fashion. Even a two-headed one can hardly be found anymore. And when you find them they are only so-so. Ah, what's the world coming to? [*Barking out sharply and abruptly to* PEER.] So it's my daughter you want.

PEER. [*Coldly.*] That's right. [*Boldly.*] And I want the kingdom too.

[*The* TROLLS *set up a mumble of indignation.*]

KING. [*Chuckling indulgently.*] You can have my daughter now, Prince Peer, and as for the kingdom, you'll get that after I'm dead.

PEER. I agree to that.

KING. But there's something else. You've got some conditions to fulfill, young man, and if you break one of them—[*Wagging a long, skinny finger at* PEER.]—the whole agreement's broken, and you won't get away from here alive.

TROLLS AND COURTIERS. [*In husky unison.*] Hanh, hanh.

KING. First you must promise to forget everything that lies outside these mountains. You must give up the sunshine and the daylight and the things people do in the day—and you must work and live in the nighttime here.

PEER. [*Nonchalantly.*] Suits me all right—if I'm king.

KING. Next, you must be able to show some wit—power to answer riddles. [*The* TROLLS *all lean toward* PEER, *listening, as the* KING *stands up from his chair to propound his riddle.*] What is the difference between a troll and a man? Tell me.

PEER. [*Thoughtfully.*] None at all. [*Grinning.*] Big trolls, I hear, will burn the hide off you and little trolls will skin you alive, and that's exactly what people do to one another in the world.

KING. [*Gleefully.*] Wonderful. And men are like trolls in something else, too. What? [*Gesturing as* PEER *is silent.*] Here among the trolls it is said, "Troll, to thyself be enough." And out there among men it is said—what?

A TROLL COURTIER. [*Sticking his long nose close by* PEER'S *ear.*] Do you see the depth of it?

ANOTHER TROLL COURTIER. [*Likewise.*] And the width of it?

A THIRD TROLL COURTIER. And the height of it?

[PEER *holds his own nose in disgust and fans the stinking air with his free hand.*]

PEER. [*Bowing before the* KING *and releasing his nose.*] Out there we say, "Look out for Number One." And that suits me to a T.

KING. Splendid, splendid. "Look out for Number One." Hmn—

PEER. Every tub must stand on its own bottom, you know. [*To the* FIRST TROLL COURTIER, *sarcastically.*] You see the depth of it? [*Then to the other two swiftly.*] And the width of it? And the height of it?

[*The* COURTIERS *laugh.*]

KING. I think I'm going to like my son-in-law. Feed him. [*He waves his hands, and two* TROLLS *wearing pigs' heads and white nightcaps run in with two trays of food and drink. The* KING *sinks back in his chair and pants forth his words, interrupted by the group of* FEMALE TROLLS *in a chord-sprung dissonance.*] The cow gives cakes and the ox gives mead.

FEMALE TROLLS. Hanh.

KING. Ask not if the taste be sour or sweet.

FEMALE TROLLS. Hanh.

KING. The important thing to remember is that these are home-made articles. No foreign trade allowed.

[*The two* PIGHEADED TROLLS *try to force the food and drink on* PEER. *He pushes them away.*]

PEER. Home-made or not—I don't like the smell.

KING. The bowl's thrown in and it's made of gold. My daughter will love a man with gold.

PEER. [*Scratches behind his ear and considers.*] There's an old saying—take the bad with the good. I suppose I can get used to drinking the stuff. [*He scratches behind his other ear and then claws at his rump with both hands. He cracks his palms together.*] It's a bargain. [*He lifts the bowl and drinks from it.*]

KING. [*Jumps up from his throne. Loudly.*] Now, courtiers, bind my Sunday tail on him.

PEER. [*Springs around and stares at him.*] What kind of foolishness is this?

KING. You can't court my daughter with a bare behind. A tail! A tail!

PEER. [*Scandalized.*] You'd turn a man into beast?

KING. [*With dignity.*] Certainly not. I'm only bringing out the true human nature inside—as men of science describe it.

PEER. [*Thoughtfully.*] Well, the scholars say man's nothing but a speck of dust. [*Shrugging his shoulders.*] So, when in Rome do as the Roman does. Animal or dust—makes no difference. [*Defiantly.*] Tie away. [*To a gabble of excitement the tail is fastened on him. The*

TROLLS *break into grunts and groans and shrill exclama-*
tions of applause and fun as PEER *swaggers and swings*
his new tail around. He stops stock-still.] What about
my religion? I was about to forget I am a church
member.

KING. Oh, keep your faith. We pride ourselves on freedom of religion here. It helps us all to do as we please.
[*Piously to* PEER.] My son, we trolls are not as black as
we are painted, and that's the true difference between
your world out there and ours here. [*Standing up from
his throne again.*] The serious business of our festival is
finished. Now let's delight our eyes and ears. [*He smacks
his hands together and the other* TROLLS *smack theirs
with him.*]

> Music maid forward,
> Let the Troll harp sound.
> Dancing maid forward,
> Let the fun begin.

[*The* MUSICIANS *step forward. In a strange and unreal
way they are similar to the musicians we have seen before—a queer female with a flute, a fellow with a misshapen violin, and another, a swollen gnome, with a lop-
sided drum. They all wear troll masks and play their
instruments in backward positions. The music they make
is dissonant and staccato, resembling in a wry manner
the music of the wedding scene. It serves both as an
accompaniment to the dancers' feet and to the husky
unison chant of vocables that sounds from the troll crew.
The* TROLL KING *reaches out and gestures* PEER *close
by him to the throne.* PEER *obeys and stands there holding his tail in his hand and beating time with it to the
music. An* OLD COURT TROLL *leers up at him.*]

OLD COURT TROLL. What you think now?

PEER. Think? Hmn. You want the truth? [*He begins clawing behind his ear with his forefinger.*]

OLD COURT TROLL. The truth, the whole truth and nothing but the truth.

PEER. I think this is a crazy crowd of folks—and ugly as sin. [*He throws back his head in a sudden insane laugh. A gap of silence falls in the music.*]

COURT TROLLS. [*With a scream.*] Eat him!

[*They charge toward* PEER. *The* KING *puts out a warding hand.*]

KING. Remember his human weakness. He is not yet able to appreciate true beauty.

TROLL VIRGINS. [*Rushing up.*] Hoo! Tear out his eyes!

[*The* GREENCLAD ONE *steps out in the middle of the scene, her back toward the throne. Bursting into loud weeping, she holds her dress up as if to catch it full of the falling tears, revealing two hairy and stocky legs.*]

GREENCLAD ONE. Hoo, hoo!

KING. [*Loudly.*] My son-in-law has been behaving most cooperatively. He has willingly drunk from the goblet of mead. He has willingly allowed a tail to be fastened on his behind. But now he is showing a touch of rebellion in not admiring these fair beauties around him. Human nature, they say, is often blind. So we must cure him. [*Softly, comforting.*] Only a slight operation is needed.

[*The* TROLLS *let loose their weird, gusty vocable again.*]

TROLLS. Hanh.

PEER. Operation?

KING. [*Pushing back his sleeves, like a surgeon ready to perform.*] In the left eye, I'll scratch you a little, then you'll see crooked—that is to say straight. Then what is really beautiful will seem so. [*An* OLD TROLL *sticks forward a glittering case of instruments.*] Now I'll cut a bit in the right pane—

[*A shiny surgeon's lancet is lifted out.*]

PEER. Oh no you don't.

KING. Then you'll realize your bride is bee-yutiful, and never will your sight be crooked again.

PEER. [*Wildly.*] He's crazy!

OLD COURT TROLL. It's you that's crazy.

KING. [*Going on complacently.*] Just think how much trouble and worry you'll be freed of. It's the way we look at things, dear son-in-law, that causes joy or sorrow. It's all in the eye.

PEER. [*Uncertainly, murmuring half to himself.*] In the Bible or somewhere it says—"If thine eye offend thee, pluck it out." [*To the* KING.] But when will I get my real sight—my human sight—back again?

KING. Never more, my son.

PEER. Oh, oh! [*Shaking his head sharply.*] Well, then, I'll have nothing to do with it. [*He starts to step away.*]

KING. Where are you going?

PEER. To get out of here.

KING. It's easy enough to get in. But the gate of the troll kingdom never opens outward. Listen now and be sensible, Prince Peer. [*Appraising him squintingly.*] You have a gift for trollship. I can see that. I'm determined to make you a troll.

PEER. [*Sulkily.*] I've put on a tail—that's true. And I've tasted your rotten liquor. But to think I'd have to stay here the rest of my life—never to be myself again—that's too much.

KING. Yourself? By all that's sinful, you make me mad. [*Hissing.*] You pale-faced dwarf. You know who I am? I'll show you who I am. First you get too free with my virgin daughter—

PEER. She's still a virgin as far as I'm concerned.

KING. You held her hot in your lust. And you've got to marry her. [PEER *snorts.*] You human beings are all the same. You think it's only deeds that count—desires and feelings go for nothing. Well, that's where you're wrong.

GREENCLAD ONE. [*Simpering.*] Peer, my love, you'll be a father when nine months are gone. [*She moves toward him to caress him.*]

PEER. [*Yelling.*] Open up! Let me out of here. [*He whirls around, wiping the sweat from his face.*]

KING. Good Prince Peer, what's done is done. Your offspring will grow up soon. Such mixed matters of body and soul thrive incredibly fast.

PEER. [*Turns pleadingly to the* GREENCLAD ONE.] I've been lying to you, lady. I have. I'm not a prince and I'm not rich. Look at me. You get poor pickings when you get me.

TROLL COURTIERS. [*Threateningly.*] Hanh!

[*The* GREENCLAD ONE *is suddenly convulsed with a pain in her stomach. Several* TROLL GIRLS *rush up ministeringly to her.*]

OLD TROLL CRONE. Your Majesty, the princess is suddenly pregnant.

KING. By all that's unholy, he's ruined her! [*He looks at* PEER *with contempt. The* MAIDENS *carry the* GREENCLAD ONE *out. The* KING *gestures fiercely toward the* COURTIERS.] Take him, children. [*He lifts his long taloned arms in a yawn.*]

TROLL BRATS. [*In singsong.*]
    O, Papa, let us first play owl and eagle,
    The wolf game and grey mouse
    And glow-eyed cat.

KING. Yes, and finish quickly. When I get angry I get sleepy. Goodnight.

[*He goes out at the right rear in the direction taken by the* GREENCLAD ONE. *He is followed by the* CHAMBERLAIN *and several of the older troll* COURTIERS. *The younger and more active ones start chasing* PEER *about the scene, pinching him.*]

PEER. [*Shrieking.*] Let me alone! You devil's imps!

[*He tries to climb up the rocks at the left but the imps pull him back.*]

TROLL BRATS. [*Squealing.*] Nixies, goblins—bite him in the rump.

PEER. [*Moans and shrieks.*] Ow! Ow!

[*He tries to run out and over the parapet at the right, but his persecutors hem him in. One of the troll brats fastens himself on* PEER'S *back and clamps his teeth on his ear.* PEER *fights at him and breaks him loose.*]

TROLL BRATS. Kill him! Kill him!

OTHER TROLL BRATS. Lock the gate, lock the gate.

[PEER *falls weeping and beaten on the ground. The* TROLLS *cover him in a heap.*]

STILL OTHER TROLL BRATS. Stomp in his face!

PEER. [*With a wild, plaintive cry.*] Mother! [*His loud call echoes beyond the rocks, and comes piteously back in a futile echo. The imps are now going to work on* PEER *in earnest.*] Solveig, Solveig! Help me, girl!

[*As if stimulated by the name of* SOLVEIG, *the church bells begin to ring far away, and the wind blows the tumbling and echoing tones across the scene.*]

TROLL BRATS. [*Shrieking in alarm.*] The bells! The church bells! Come away—away—away-y!

[*They flee howling back in among the rocks. The scene darkens swiftly. The low, steady beat of the drum is heard far off, measured now in the thumping heartbeat of the frightened* PEER *as he lies on the ground. He crawls weakly to his feet, picks up a broken branch of a tree to steady himself. He thrashes about him at imaginary and enveloping terrors. His motions are now enervated and dream-like, almost like one wading in a stream of deep water.*

The wind, filled with the eerie, indistinguishable voices of the subsiding trolls, rises in the hollow void at the rear

*and becomes the deep bellows-breathing of some prime-
val creature—living, real, but formless and unseen. The
breathing goes and comes, dies, is reborn again.* PEER
*moans in his nerveless terror and beats slowly about him
like a blind man, like one whose sense of equilibrium has
become unstable and faulty. His breath finally breaks
through his lips as if from congested and explosive
lungs.*]

PEER. [*Challenging the breather.*] Who are you?

[*He waits, the darkness answers him—a voice which
might be the tongueless mouth of the stage itself, an in-
choate and terrifying presence, heard and felt but not
seen. The drum continues its beating in the void, like the
thumping of* PEER'S *heart.*]

VOICE. Myself.

PEER. [*Lunging and spinning.*] Get out of my way! [*He
strikes in front of him, then behind him.*]

VOICE. Go around, Peer. There's room enough.

PEER. [*As before.*] Who are you?

VOICE. Myself. [*The silence is intense and frightful.*]
Who are *you?*

PEER. [*Suffocatingly, as if his head were wrapped in a
quilt.*] Me, Peer Gynt! And my sword can cut, I tell you!
Hey! Now I'll slash your heart out. [*He lifts his branch
and strikes and chops the air feebly.*] Who are you?

VOICE. Myself.

PEER. That crazy answer! Who are you?

VOICE. [*With a huge, frog-like gulp.*] The great ogre.

PEER. [*Butting forward.*] Get out of my way, you ogre!

VOICE. Go roundabout, Peer!

PEER. Straight through, I tell you! [*He lurches here and there and butts the air. He strikes and chops but is pushed back by the invisible creature. He blinks benumbed at the branch.*] The trolls have conjured my sword. But I have my fists. [*He throws the branch behind him and begins beating at the enemy with his fists.*]

VOICE. That's right, trust your fists, Peer Gynt. Hee— hee! And you'll climb to the top.

PEER. [*Croakingly, hypnotically.*] Backwards and forwards, it's all the same. There he is and there he is. Let me see you. What kind of thing are you?

VOICE. The ogre.

PEER. [*Screaming.*] Fight back at me! [*He attacks the air again.*]

VOICE. The ogre never fights.

PEER. I'll make you.

VOICE. The great ogre wins without fighting. The great ogre wins all and strikes no blow.

[*A wild flapping of bird wings is heard flying and circling in the darkness above* PEER'S *now illuminated and maddened form. A medley of shrill voices, high, weird and aerial accompanies the flapping.* PEER *falls on his knees, his hands outstretched in piteous pleading before the invisible and frustrating power.*]

BIRD SCREAMS. [*From the air above.*] Have you got him, Ogre?

VOICE. He's coming—step by step.

[PEER *is pulled along on his knees toward the precipice void at the back, pulled along by the suction of a strange mesmeric force. His hands are still outstretched, his face raised toward heaven.*]

BIRD SCREAMS. [*In echoing weird summons.*] Sisters, sisters, far away. Come forth to the feast.

[*The drumming of bird wings increases, mingled with the drumbeat of* PEER'S *heart and the drum beating beyond the rocks.*]

PEER. [*Sobbingly.*] Save me, Solveig! Solveig! Solveig! [*He falls forward on his face, his body wriggling toward the precipice.*]

BIRD SCREAMS. He is weakening.

VOICE. We've got him!

BIRD SCREAMS. Sisters, hurry, hurry! [*Shrieking triumphantly.*] Ogre! Take him! Take him!

[*A whining sob of terror comes up out of* PEER'S *belly. Church bells begin ringing again far in the mountains, drawing nearer, a psalm sung by many voices rising above them. Now we hear the psalm led by the voice of a girl singing. It is* SOLVEIG'S *voice. The flapping of the bird wings weakens, the outlandish shrill cries fade. The voice of the ogre dies in a great blopping gulp.*]

VOICE. He was too strong. A woman's love has helped him.

[*The psalm singing comes nearer, louder.* SOLVEIG *appears from the left rear, a radiant vision.* PEER *staggers to his feet. The light brightens. And now over at the right front we see the* BUTTONMOLDER *standing forth from the rock. He starts toward* PEER *whose entranced gaze is on the vision of* SOLVEIG. SOLVEIG'S *form moves across the scene toward the right, beckoningly.* PEER *stumbles after her. The* BUTTONMOLDER *turns away, and the light fades from the scene. The singing swells up more loudly, the voice of* SOLVEIG *high and clear.*]

VOICES. [*Chanting, led by* SOLVEIG'S *voice.*]

The earth is the Lord's and all that therein is.
The compass of the world and they that dwell therein.
For he hath founded it upon the seas
And prepareth it upon the floods.

[*The light fades.*]

Who shall ascend into the hill of the Lord
Or who shall rise up in his holy place?

[*The light dies out. The chanting continues.*]

PART ONE

Scene V

High up in the rugged mountains. At the right rear against the rock stands a little pioneer hut. Over the door is a spread of reindeer horns, exaggerated as to shape and size—symbolic of life and vitality. Beyond the hut is a vista of mountains, fold on fold, and in one of these folds is a little chaliced lake, green-frozen and mirrored. The blue twilight of a still and frost-gripped evening is coming on. And a feeling of snow is everywhere.

PEER GYNT is in front of the hut working at a wooden door bar with his axe. SOLVEIG, wrapped in her shawl, her face pale and pure and yet troubled, is hovering helpfully around him. She grasps her little white prayer book in one hand. PEER is more unkempt, unshaven and wild eyed than ever. He knocks and trims away at the bar, trying to ignore SOLVEIG.

PEER. [*Speaking to himself.*] There'll have to be a lock —to shut the door from people—and from the trolls. [*Glancing out from under his shaggy brow.*] And what about something to keep out bad thoughts? [*He cuts a sharp look at* SOLVEIG.] They creep about and squeeze in, you know. [*Speaking harshly and mockingly at him-*

self.] You're a fool, Peer Gynt—if you think bars and bolts can keep a man from thinking.

[*He strikes the bar a spiteful blow with the axe. It bounces over to one side.* SOLVEIG *bends quickly to lift it for him, but he jerks it away from her sullenly.*]

SOLVEIG. You shouldn't reject my love, Peer. I felt you wanted me. So I came, and so you must take me.

PEER. [*Stops the motion of his axe and stares at her.*] Seems you'd be afraid to come up here—to me.

SOLVEIG. [*Her head nodding in anguish.*] The nights and the days were heavy and empty. Life was dead down there. [*She gestures slightly with her little prayer book toward the valley below.*] I couldn't laugh. I couldn't cry. I only knew you wanted me.

PEER. [*Leans on his axe, his eyes fastened on her.*] But your father—

SOLVEIG. I have no one to call Father—or Mother any more.

PEER. [*Keeps looking at her as she stands in the lonely twilight, sweet, piteous, and devoted. As his mood begins to melt under the warm influence of her faith and love, a gentle radiance illuminates the air around her— the way he sees her in his fevered imagination. Suddenly tremulous.*] Solveig—

SOLVEIG. You must be everything to me now. [*Tearfully.*] It was sad to part with my little sister. It was worse even to part from my father—but worst of all from my mother. [*Shaking her head.*] No, God forgive me. It was one sorrow to part from them all.

PEER. [*Takes a step toward her as if to enclose her in his powerful and uncouth arms, then stops.*] You know the sentence of the law against me. I am declared an outlaw.

SOLVEIG. [*Gently.*] So you need me.

PEER. [*Loudly.*] Outside of the forest anyone can take me. There's a price on my head.

SOLVEIG. [*Murmurously.*] They asked where I was going—and I answered, going home. [*She grows more warm and radiant before* PEER's *sight.*]

PEER. [*Jubilantly.*] You dare live here with this hunter— [*Tapping his breast.*]—with me? [*She gazes at him, her eyes trusting and tearful. He murmurs ecstatically.*] Solveig, let me look at you—not too close—just look at you— How light and fair you are! [*He sweeps her up hungrily in his arms, gazing down at her face.*] I'll not hurt you. I'll hold you out from me—lovely and warm. I'll keep you safe. [*He lowers her to the ground. She clings to him.*] Who would have thought you ever could love me? [*He caresses her and kisses the top of her hair.*] Ay, but I've wanted you night and day.

SOLVEIG. Down there I felt myself stifling. But here where one listens to the pine trees whispering—here I am—home.

PEER. [*Earnestly.*] And you are sure in your heart, Solveig—for all your days you are sure?

SOLVEIG. [*Lifting her eyes to him.*] The way I have come—can never lead back.

PEER. [*Softly, intensely.*] Now you are mine. [*He leads her toward the door of the little hut, then stops.*] Go in.

I'll fetch wood for the fire. And it'll burn warm and bright. And you'll never be cold. [*He gestures toward the door. It opens as of itself before* SOLVEIG. *She goes in looking back at him. The door closes itself.* PEER *stands a moment quietly and then laughs a gay, loud laugh and leaps into the air.*] She is my true princess!

[*He grasps his axe. The day has deepened into full twilight save for an illumination on the little door—as if* SOLVEIG'S *presence there behind it sheds gold into the air. Now from within the cabin we hear* SOLVEIG'S *voice raised in her song of love and content. We only get the melody, the words are indistinct.* PEER *lifts his head, his axe in the air, entranced. The song dies away as if some inimical influence were entering the scene and causing it to fade. At the right front now we see the evil influence—a slatternly* ELDERLY WOMAN *in a dirty green dress. With her is a big ugly* BRAT *limping along holding onto her skirt and carrying a beer mug in one grimy hand and a small axe tucked under his arm.*]

GREENCLAD ONE. Good evening.

PEER. [*Suddenly shivering, alert.*] Who's that?

GREENCLAD ONE. Old friends, Peer Gynt. My house is close by.

PEER. [*Sharply, still not looking around.*] I don't know you.

GREENCLAD ONE. Have you forgot the evening at my father's house when you drank the mead? Have you forgot— [*To the* BRAT.] Give your father a drink.

PEER. [*Springs around and gazes at the woman and brat in horror.*] Father!

GREENCLAD ONE. [*Waddling ingratiatingly forward.*] Surely you know your own son. Can't you see he's lame —lame in the leg like you are lame in the soul.

PEER. [*Lifting his axe threateningly.*] This spindle-shanked bastard!

GREENCLAD ONE. He's grown up fast.

PEER. You troll snout! You can't father that thing on me. [*The* GREENCLAD ONE *bursts into tears.*]

GREENCLAD ONE. How can I help that I'm no longer pretty. Last fall when I gave birth, the devil squeezed me—so there's a reason I've turned so ugly. [*Leering at him and plying her coarse wiles.*] But if you want to see me all pretty again, just turn the girl in there outdoors. Kick her out of your heart and mind. Do that, sweetheart, and I'll shed my snout.

PEER. [*Yelling.*] Get away from me, you troll witch!

GREENCLAD ONE. [*Clutches his arm.*] Ah, no, my darling.

PEER. [*Trying to pull away from her.*] I'll crack your head.

GREENCLAD ONE. Ho-ho, Peer Gynt, I don't mind a beating. [PEER *jerks loose from her. He draws his axe threateningly back. She lurches away, holding the* BRAT *by the hand. She turns around.*] I'll be back here every blessed day. I will. [*Venomously.*] I'll listen at the door and spy on you both. If you get loving, Peer Gynt, if you coax and caress her—[*Cackling.*]—I'll push in close and demand my share. We two will swap and use you between us.

PEER. Scat, you hellcat!

GREENCLAD ONE. Little devil, speak to your father.

BRAT. [*Springs forward, spits at* PEER *and flies back to his mother.*] Phooey.

GREENCLAD ONE. [*Kissing the* BRAT.] What a head he's got on his shoulders! The spit and image of his father.

PEER. [*Despairingly.*] It's a lie.

GREENCLAD ONE. See what comes of your lust and your lechery.

PEER. [*Calling brokenly toward the little hut.*] Solveig—

GREENCLAD ONE. Oh, yes, it's the innocent get hurt! [*Weeping.*] And I was innocent like her.

[*The* BRAT *suddenly throws the beer mug at* PEER. *The woman takes him by the hand and the two of them go away among the rocks at the right rear.* PEER *stands shamed and crushed. He glances apprehensively toward the little hut. The radiance and glory have now disappeared from the door. He bows his head in a groan, starts halfheartedly toward the door and then his feet stop again.*]

PEER. [*Muttering.*] Go around, said the Voice. [*The little hut is now fading out in the deepening twilight.* PEER *drops his hands helplessly.*] A wall's closed up around her. Everything's turned ugly and old all of a sudden. [*Fiercely advising himself.*] There's Scripture for repentance. But what—what is it? I can't remember. [*Wagging his head.*] Repentance? [*He shakes his head, a sigh going out of him.*] A man shouldn't walk

where the grass grows green—the school teacher said.
[*He gazes off in the direction taken by the woman and
the brat.*] That old hag was lying. [*He turns his face
away and closes his eyes.*] Now all that ugliness is gone
out of my sight. It's gone. [*Ragingly.*] Yes, out of
sight—[*He turns toward the door in a frenzy of indeci-
sion.*]—but not out of my mind. [*Balling up his fists and
straightening his shoulders in resolution.*] I've got to get
around this somehow. [*He thinks, and feels better in
his soul already as he thinks. He will strike a middle
ground. He will enjoy* SOLVEIG *and yet not soil her love.
He starts into the hut, foul as he is, and then out of his
soul comes the hateful thought and image—the* GREEN-
CLAD ONE *and the ugly* BRAT. PEER *is struck back by his
sins surging in him. The melody of* SOLVEIG'S *song rises
in the hut, weak and pleading and begging withal. The
song is answered once more in* PEER'S *soul by the leering
laugh of the* GREENCLAD ONE *and the spitting syllable of
the* BRAT. *Purity calls to* PEER. *Impurity ferments within
him. The purity in him fights the impurity and gives
him his impulse. He moves away from the hut.*] Ugly
and filthy with sin? Go in with all these trolls hanging
on me—? [*Pierced by an image.*] And Ingrid. And the
three girls in the hills. They'll crowd in too and beg
their share—and me holding her in my arms.

[*The struggle in him rages. Sweat pours down and he
wipes his forehead with his ragged sleeve. The door to
the little hut opens and* SOLVEIG *stands there. But her
dress is dull and the color of ashes now.*]

I could never put her down pure again. [*Gesturing helplessly.*] Out there somewhere—not power, not gold—a
man might cleanse himself—forget these slimy evil
things— Ah.

SOLVEIG. I'm waiting, Peer.

PEER. [*Holds his axe in his hand, not looking around. Loudly and into the air.*] Round about.

SOLVEIG. What is it, Peer?

PEER. [*Feeling for words.*] You must keep waiting. [*Brokenly, anguished.*] It's dark now. I've got a heavy load to fetch.

SOLVEIG. I will help you. We'll carry it together.

PEER. [*Bitterly, but still without looking around.*] Stay where you are. I'll carry it alone. [*He starts out of the scene at the left front.*]

SOLVEIG. I want to help you, Peer.

PEER. [*Roughly.*] I've got to do it myself, I tell you.

SOLVEIG. What, Peer? [*She reaches her hands for him.*]

PEER. Be patient, girl, and wait for me.

[*He turns and gazes at her forlornly and yet somewhat defiantly. For an instant he stands so.* SOLVEIG *slowly nods her head, comprehending him, resolute in the strength that her true love gives.*]

SOLVEIG. Yes, I'll wait.

[PEER *hurries along the woodpath out at the left front, carrying his axe in his hand.* SOLVEIG *remains standing in the open door a moment, then she slowly turns back into the hut. The door closes slowly behind her. Far away the drum beat is heard, spurting up with new energy as if stimulated by its quarry coming its way. The light fades out and the drum continues beating.*]

PART ONE

Scene VI

The little room in AASE'S *house. It is night.* AASE, *dressed in an old white nightgown, is twisting and turning on her bed of weakness and pain.*

AASE. [*Feverishly.*] Why don't Peer come? Why don't he come? [*She tries to sit up.*] I've got no one to send word to him. There's so much I've got to tell him. My time is growing short. [*She gradually gets her feet from the bed and pushes herself up, hoping to make her way to the door to call for help.*] Peer! Peer! [*Her old nightgown hangs down straight about her. She starts shuffling across the floor, then staggers, grips the back of her chair, hangs on, and collapses to the floor with a groan. She lies there in a faint of dead weakness.*]
PEER. [*Enters from the right rear, still carrying his axe in his hand. Looking about him and addressing the empty room.*] Mother. [*No answer comes to his greeting. He fails to see* AASE'S *form sprawled in the shadows behind the chair. He rummages along in a chest at the foot of the bed, pulls out an old jacket and swiftly puts it on, and then a cap, then a pair of snowshoes. He is hurrying to escape out of the scene. He opens the little window, looks out and calls.*] Mother! [*But only the drum in the distance answers him, coming in a little more loudly now.* PEER *closes the window sharply and*

71

seizes a loaf of bread from the cupboard. He takes a huge and hungry mouthful, stuffs the loaf into his shirt and crams a piece of sausage and cheese into his pocket. He knocks over a long-handled casting ladle leaning against the wall. He picks it up and stares at it. A half smile of remembrance moves about his tense lips.] Hello, old molding ladle. I used to play buttonmaker with you, melting and molding and stamping buttons. [*He turns the ladle in his hand and sets it back against the wall. He sees his mother's form on the floor. With a cry he drops down beside her. The sound of the drum is heard more loudly.* PEER *springs to his feet again, reaching for his snowshoes to flee. Once more he is in the throes of a moral battle—as he was in front of the little hut in the mountains. And again his better nature wins. He lays aside the shoes, takes off his cap, bends down and lifts his mother up in his arms and puts her on the bed. He strokes her hands, rubs her forehead, pats her, glancing apprehensively off in the direction of the fatal and remorseless oncoming law symbolized in the sound of the drum.*]

AASE. [*Opens her eyes. Tremulously.*] The Lord bless you with his grace! So you've come, my dear, dear boy. [*Fearfully, clinging to him.*] But how dare you come down to the valley? You know your life's at stake here!

PEER. [*Soothingly.*] Never mind about my life. I had to look in a bit to see you.

AASE. And now I can die in peace.

PEER. Die? What's all this foolishness?

AASE. [*Breathing heavily.*] Ah, Peer, I'm coming to the end. My hour is nigh.

PEER. [*Clucks at her cheeringly and rubs her face. Finally.*] Your feet and hands are cold. [*He rubs her more swiftly.*]

AASE. Aye, Peer, it will soon be over. When you see my eyes grow filled with death, you must close them carefully. And take good care to see to my coffin. Let it be a nice one, dear.

PEER. There's plenty of time to think of that. Now we'll talk together—but only light and silly talk—and forget everything that's wrong and ugly, and everything that's nasty and mean. [*He moves swiftly about the bed now, making her comfortable.*] Are you thirsty? Can I get you a drink? This bed's too short. [*Jollying her.*] It was mine as a boy. [*He sits down and strokes her forehead again.*] You remember how you used to come at night and sit by me here, and spread the blanket all snug over me and sing me ballads and baby songs?

AASE. [*Whispering.*] Fetch me the Bible there. I'm feeling so restless in my mind.

PEER. And tell me stories—such foolish stories—the one about the thread balls—and how they talked to their father, the spool?

AASE. The Good Book is my comfort—my rod and my staff.

PEER. And the wild blowing autumn leaves that spoke to the murderer and made him confess.

AASE. [*Murmuring.*] The Bible, Peer.

PEER. [*Reaches around and picks up the Bible. He holds it an instant in his hand and then lays it quickly aside as if the touch of it disturbs him. Gazing far off.*] And the game we used to play—you remember that? How we'd drive our fiery horses! [*Buoyantly.*] Listen! In the Soria-Moria castle a feast is given by the Prince and King. Now you rest yourself on the sleigh cushion. I will drive you there. [*He pulls a piece of rope from the closet and throws it over the back of the chair. He sits on the chair in front of his propped-up mother and begins driving an imaginary sleigh.*]

AASE. [*Childishly.*] But, dear Peer, am I invited to the castle?

PEER. [*Heartily.*] Of course you're invited. You always were. [*He waves his whip in the air.*] Giddup. Shake a leg there, Blackie.

[*He jiggles his rope reins and clucks. The distant drum is a little nearer now, more threatening, and the faint halloos of the posse echo in the mountains. PEER listens but still drives his mother determinedly on toward glory.*]

AASE. I hear a sound of ringing.

PEER. It's the shiny harness bells, Mother mine.

AASE. [*As the drum sounds nearer.*] Hoo, how hollow it sounds.

PEER. We are driving over the fiord, Mother. The ice is hollow and rumbles.

AASE. I'm scared. What is it that hums so strangely?

[*The vocables of the approaching neighbors are sounding nearer.*]

PEER. It is the pine trees, Mother, singing in the wind. Just rest quietly. [*He cracks his whip and clucks to his chair steed.*]

AASE. Something sparkles and glitters away there. Where does that light come from?

[*Beams from the neighbors' lanterns are seen weaving and wavering up the valley at the back.*]

PEER. From the castle windows, Mother. Can you hear? Listen to the dancing.

AASE. [*Quivering with joy.*] Yes.

PEER. Outside Saint Peter is standing—I can see him. He's inviting you to stop and come inside.

AASE. [*Wonderingly.*] Inviting me?

PEER. Aye, with honor.

AASE. Oh, dear, Peer, what fancy doings you're driving your poor old mother to!

PEER. [*Snapping the whip.*] Giddup, will you hurry, Blackie?

AASE. You drive so fast! It makes me weary.

PEER. [*Pointing.*] There, see the castle shining all lighted up before us. Our drive now will soon be over.

AASE. [*Snugly.*] I'll lie now and close my eyes and put my faith in you, dear boy.

PEER. [*Gazing ahead.*] Ooh, there's a big crowd at the castle. The people are all milling around at the gate. [*Imitatively, simulating a dialogue.*] Here comes Peer Gynt with his mother. What say you, Mr. Saint Peter?

Can my mother come in here? You'd have to look a long time before you'd find a more honest soul. As for myself now, the less said about Peer Gynt the better. But you must count it an honor to have her here. And please you, sir, make her happy. You won't find anyone from down home better than she is. Ho, ho, there comes God the Father. Saint Peter, now you're going to catch it. [*With a deep voice.*] Stop being so proud and choosy, Peter. Mother Aase is welcome here. [*He laughs loudly and turns around to his mother.*] That's just what I knew would happen. [*He stops his jiggling, rises from the chair, frightened. The posse is near at hand now, the lantern lights flashing menacingly.*] Your eyes, Mother —your eyes! Why do you look like that? [*Calling loudly.*] Mother! [*He goes to the head of the bed.*] Don't lie there and stare at me. Speak—Mother!—it's me—your boy Peer. [*He reaches out gently and touches her forehead, then her hands. He speaks softly.*] I see. [*To the chair.*] You can rest yourself now. Our ride is over. [*He bends down and reverently closes* AASE'S *eyes.*] I thank you now for all your days—for lickings and for the kisses of my childhood. But see, you must thank me back. [*He presses his cheek against her mouth.*] There—I'm repaid for everything.

[*The noise of a gate slamming is heard off scene.* PEER *springs up and stands still, his hands hanging down. He has waited too late. He will be taken now. But the posse has not yet arrived. Several neighboring women come slowly in the scene,* KARI, *the cotter's wife, in front. They are all wrapped in heavy dark shawls. Among them is* SOLVEIG. *The cotter's wife comes over toward* PEER. *She sees him and starts back with an exclamation of surprise and fear.*]

KARI. Peer! [*Recognition comes over* PEER. *It is not the law. The tense apprehensiveness dissolves away. He breathes a deep sigh.* KARI *approaches the bed.*] Good Lord, how well she sleeps.

PEER. Hush, she's dead. [*A gasp goes out of* KARI. *She kneels down weeping by the bed. The other* WOMEN *kneel in the yard outside.* PEER *stands a moment in thought and then speaks.*] Get Mother buried in a good grave. [*He turns his head, listening, then picks up his axe and snowshoes.*] I'll try to get away.

SOLVEIG. Are you going far?

PEER. [*A tremor goes through* PEER *at the sound of her voice, but he keeps his face averted.*] Toward the ocean.

SOLVEIG. So far? [*Her shawl drops back, her face revealed.*]

[PEER *strides toward the right front, then stops and stands still a moment.*]

PEER. And farther still.

SOLVEIG. [*Softly, intensely.*] Why, Peer, why?

PEER. I'll find the answer myself.

[*He throws his axe behind him, symbolic of freeing himself of Norway, his homeland. Then he slings his snowshoes over his shoulder and plunges out at the right front.* SOLVEIG *moves a step or two after him. She picks up the fallen axe and holds it to her. The dark figure of the* BUTTONMOLDER *is seen now in the rear of the room. He takes the casting ladle in his hand and goes out of the scene, following* PEER. *By this time the posse with the loudly beaten drum and lanterns is beginning to come in. Near the head of the group is* INGRID. *She is tenderly accompanied by* MADS MOEN. *We recognize in the posse the people of the wedding scene.* KARI *and several of the old women are kneeling down around the bed where the body of* AASE *lies with the light spilling on it. The noise of the posse and the beaten drum are suddenly silenced at the fact of death. The people kneel down. Over at the right front,* SOLVEIG *kneels, her face lifted in the direction* PEER *has gone.* SOLVEIG'S FATHER, *ministerial and grave, remains standing. He lifts his hands in benediction over the scene.*]

THE PEOPLE. [*Led by* SOLVEIG'S FATHER, *chanting reverently and softly in respect to the dead.*]

> Man that is born of woman
> Is of few days
> And full of trouble.
> He cometh forth like a flower
> And is cut down.
> He fleeth as a shadow
> And continueth not.

[*The scene fades out as the chanting continues and dies.*]

INTERMISSION

PART TWO

PART TWO

SCENE I

The southwest coast of Morocco. A few palm trees show in the scene at the left rear. A hammock is strung between two of them. Downstage a little to the right, a table is set for a sumptuous meal. Straw mats are on the ground. Two ATTENDANTS *in eastern costume do the serving. In the distance at the rear we see the blue of the Mediterranean Sea, and there anchored offshore is the bright, shapely form of a ship, Peer Gynt's steam yacht, showing a Norwegian and an American flag. In the middle background at the edge of the sea, a dinghy is pulled up partly on the sand. It is near sundown.*

*Seated around the table are four men of different nationalities—*MR. COTTON, MONSIEUR BALLON, HERR VON EBERKOPF *and* HERR TRUMPETERSTRAALE. *They are drinking deeply and dining plentifully.*

MONSIEUR BALLON. Monsieur Peer Gynt is communing with—er—ah—himself.

HERR VON EBERKOPF. The desert is a fitting place for it.

MR. COTTON. Sir Peer Gynt, he calls himself.

EBERKOPF. Lord Peer Gynt.

81

HERR TRUMPETERSTRAALE. He behaves like a king.

COTTON. [*Calling off.*] Your hospitality is wonderful, sir.

PEER. [*In the distance.*] Delighted, gentlemen, delighted.

BALLON. [*Chuckling.*] The man that walks alone. [*Shaking his head.*] What he thinks, *je ne sais pas.*

COTTON. But what he has—we know. [*He gestures toward the ship in the distance.*]

EBERKOPF. Gold—gold.

TRUMPETERSTRAALE. In the bottom of that ship—yellow gold.

[*The* FOUR MEN *as if moved by one concerted will put their heads together.*]

EBERKOPF. Let him walk farther in the desert.

BALLON. Shh-shh.

[*The* ATTENDANTS *come forward to pour more wine and then retire.*]

COTTON. Let him eat and drink—then in the hammock a siesta.

[*They all nod.*]

ALL. [*Ad lib.*] Yes. Ja. Oui.

[*They look off and then devote themselves to their food with bowed heads.* PEER *comes strolling in from the right. He is a handsome middle-aged man in elegant travelling clothes, with a gold pince nez hanging from a black silk cord around his neck. He wears a well-trimmed*

*beard and carries an umbrella under his arm. Stopping,
he considers the four men with a jovial look.*]

PEER. Drink, gentlemen. Eat, gentlemen. [*The four men
rise quickly to their feet, bow to him and at his gesture
reseat themselves.*] If man was made for pleasure, then
let him have pleasure. [*Gesturing over the table.*] What
else may I offer you?

[*They all shake their heads, signifying they are completely satisfied. One of the attendants rushes up and
pours PEER a great tumbler of wine. He drains it off with
a flourish, a flourish typical of PEER in this stage of his
life—the egocentric cutting his swath in the world.*]

TRUMPETERSTRAALE. You are superb as a host, Your
Excellency.

PEER. My money is the host—not I. Be thankful to it.
[*Indicating the two ATTENDANTS.*] And to my cook and
steward.

COTTON. [*Lifting his glass.*] A toast to our good luck—
the luck of us four.

PEER. [*Chuckling.*] With me there are five.

[*The FOUR MEN laugh vapidly and lift their glasses in a
toast.*]

BALLON. Monsieur, you have a *gout,* a *ton*— [*Pinching
the air with ladylike fingers.*] A taste exquiseete—that
nowadays is rarely found— [*Fatuously.*] A certain *je
ne sais quoi*—

EBERKOPF. [*Grandiosely.*] He is the successful man of
the world—liberated—free—not bound by narrow

prejudices—but stamped with lofty understanding—the wisdom of life.

[PEER *chuckles again and shrugs his shoulders. He digs* EBERKOPF *in the side with a sharp forefinger and holds his glass out again. The* ATTENDANT *steps quickly up, refills it, and* PEER *drinks.*]

BALLON. *Oui, oui.* But when we say it in French it sounds more beautiful—*l'homme de la liberte!*

EBERKOPF. *Ja.* But French is so stiff—so Gallic! [*Leaning toward* PEER *and staring up in his face.*] How did you become so successful, Sir Peter Gynt?

PEER. [*Jovially.*] Well, gentlemen, because I never married.

THE FOUR. [*Ad lib.*] Clever. Excellent. The perfect answer.

PEER. You know I am lying. [*Shaking his head.*] The reason, gentlemen, is I have been myself. [*After a pause.*] My advice to you is brief and to the point. A man should always be himself. [*He picks up a piece of roast with a delicate gesture, stares at it, and then takes a great wolfish bite of it. His mouth stuffed, he flings the bone back onto the table, reaches over, jerks a voluminous white handkerchief from* TRUMPETERSTRAALE'S *pocket, wipes his hands, and then returns the handkerchief.*] Look after Number One, that's it.

[*He taps himself on the chest.* COTTON *gestures an* ATTENDANT *forward, and* PEER'S *glass is filled again.*]

COTTON. Simply wonderful.

PEER. Remember, it's the sharp blade that cuts deep and truly. I have kept myself sharpened.

EBERKOPF. [*Peering at his glass.*] But this being yourself—

PEER. Of and for myself—

EBERKOPF. I am sure has cost you quite a struggle.

PEER. The strong man wins. The weak go down. [*He throws his empty glass from him. The* ATTENDANT *catches it expertly.* PEER *is slightly drunk. He wanders over to the hammock at the left rear and sits down. The* SECOND ATTENDANT *comes out of the shadows carrying a lute in his hand. He squats on the sand by the hammock and starts to play.* PEER *lifts his hand and the music subsides.*] Once, though, I was nearly caught—in a trap against my will.

BALLON. [*Snickering.*] A woman.

PEER. Never put your head in a woman's lap, gentlemen.

TRUMPETERSTRAALE. Never trust a woman, hah, hah!

PEER. Exactly. [*He swings his feet up in the hammock and lies back, his hands clasped behind his head, gazing up at the stars. The* FIRST ATTENDANT *puts a cigar quickly into his mouth and strikes a match to it.* PEER *puffs and tastes the fine tobacco savoringly. The slave with the lute resumes his playing. The* FOUR MEN *at the table put their heads together in a further confidence. The shadows deepen down on* PEER'S *hammock. But at the sound of his voice the* FOUR MEN *straighten up again.*] It's fate that rules a man's life, gentlemen. [*Blowing smoke in a cloud.*] And it's a comforting thing to know.

EBERKOPF. [*Stands up and addresses* PEER *stiffly and punctiliously.*] You have a view of life, sir, and life's ways, which raises you to the rank of a great thinker—while an ordinary fellow—[*Indicating himself.*]—like me sees each thing by itself and never stops fumbling. You understand how to connect all things together.

COTTON. With the same yardstick we measure everything, but you, sir, point up each loose observation into a separate fact—like rays from the light of your life's philosophy. [*Abruptly.*] And you have never gone to college?

[EBERKOPF *sits down.*]

PEER. [*From his hammock, laconically.*] I am, as I have told you before, a simple and self-made man. I never learned anything by method, gentlemen. History I got piecemeal. And then since a man must put faith in something, I took on religion—by fits and starts.

COTTON. That was practical.

[*The* OTHERS *nod.*]

EBERKOPF. It pays to be safe.

PEER. [*Swings his feet out from the hammock and sits up.*] When first I went to the west there—to America—I was a poor fellow with empty hands. I sweated hard to get my food, I tell you. [*He stands suddenly up and steadies himself, using his umbrella as a walking stick. The light brightens on him.*] Life, dear friends, is a sweet thing. And as they say, death's a bitter pill. Between them you steer your way. And luck was with me. [*Glancing up at the sky.*] And old Fate—[*Lifting his umbrella and pointing.*]—up there, or wherever he is, was with me. [*He stands listening, his face uplifted. Somewhere in the depths of the sky there is a faint thundery rumble as in the opening of the play.* PEER *hears it and smiles. The* FOUR MEN *sense it and are troubled. The* TWO ATTENDANTS, *apparently hearing nothing, care nothing.*] I prospered. I worked harder. I prospered more. [*Stepping over toward the group emphatically, the heady wine making his tongue free.*] In ten years I bore the name of Croesus among the Charleston shipowners. My reputation was high in every port, and luck rode with my ships.

[*He is at the table.* COTTON *proffers him another full glass of wine.* PEER *takes it and drinks deeply. The* FOUR YESMEN *look at him with smiling, honeyed faces.*]

COTTON. What did you deal in?

PEER. Negroes—Negroes to Carolina. And idols to China.

BALLON. Incredible.

TRUMPETERSTRAALE. The devil, Uncle Gynt!

PEER. You might say the business hovered on the shady side. But believe me, once begun these things are hard to quit. You get a monopoly which employs thousands of people—you can't suddenly quit and turn them out of work. [*He snaps his fingers. The* FOUR *nod in agreement.* PEER *drops heavily down into a chair and leans over on the table toward them.*] But then you have to watch out for what you might call—the consequences. [*He laughs and slaps the table jocosely with the butt of his hand. The* OTHERS *laugh and strike the table in soft imitation likewise.*] Yet I've always hated to wind things up. But nature doesn't. She invented the grave, you know. Well, I was beginning to age. I kept thinking to myself—who knows how soon my hour will strike? I decided to put my house in order. It's best to be on the right side.

TRUMPETERSTRAALE. True, true.

[*The* OTHERS *nod.*]

PEER. But what could I do? To stop the trade with China was impossible. But where there's a will there's a way. I opened up another trade at the same time with China. Every spring I exported idols. And every fall I sent missionaries to the same country. I outfitted them with what they needed—with stockings, Bibles, rum and rice. [*He wags his head.*]

COTTON. [*Chuckling.*] But at a profit.

PEER. Of course. And the scheme worked. For every idol I disposed of, the missionaries saved a coolie's soul. They know this system well in America—lend to one hand so that the other can buy. [*The* FOUR *shake with appreciative laughter.*] It paid good dividends. The more idols I sent, the more missionaries were required to preach.

COTTON. [*Greedily.*] And the slaves you trafficked in?

PEER. [*With fine irony.*] There once more my moral sense won out. I began to feel this traffic was, as I said, on the shady side. [*Winking.*] I quit the slave trade and bought holdings in the South. I kept the last boatload of Africans for my own use. They grew greasy fat and in the prime. [*Somewhat drunkenly now.*] I was a kind of father to them. At the proper time I sold out—every piece of chattel, livestock, hide and hair. I gave the men and women drink and the widows plenty of snuff. [*He stands up, steadies himself by the table and continues.*] There's an old proverb—who does no ill does good. So my former sins are forgiven and I keep my head unbowed.

[*The* FOUR *touch their glasses to* PEER's *and drink. He tosses his glass carelessly aside again. The* ATTENDANT *catches it.*]

EBERKOPF. [*Enthusiastically.*] How refreshing it is to hear a life philosophy and see it acted out—no fog of theorizing, no bringing in of outside issues—right to the point—the hard fact and the deed.

PEER. [*Who has started wandering toward his hammock again, turns back.*] The whole secret of success, my friends, is to have the courage of one's action—the will to act. [*Lifting a forefinger admonishingly.*] Always keep a bridge open behind you over which you can retreat. That's an old Norwegian saying, and I've remembered it. [*He starts on toward his hammock.*]

[BALLON *jiggles* COTTON's *sleeve.* COTTON *calls after* PEER.]

COTTON. Very edifying, sir. But another little matter— we are curious to know—what you plan to do with all your gold?

PEER. [*Stopping.*] Do, hey?

THE FOUR. [*In unison, leaning forward.*] Yes, tell us.

PEER. [*Turning around, sticking his umbrella in the sand and resting his hands on the knob.*] Well, just what

we are doing—travel. [*Confidentially.*] You see, gentlemen, that's why I took you on board as bosom cronies at
Gibraltar. [*Sarcastically.*] I needed such a chorus as you
fellows to dance around my golden calf.

[*The* FOUR *look at one another.*]

TRUMPETERSTRAALE. [*Wiping his lips with his rumpled
handkerchief.*] Very wittily said, sir.

[*With the exception of* COTTON, *the others nod.*]

COTTON. But a man just doesn't raise his sails simply
to be sailing. You must have some plan in mind—some
purpose.

PEER. I always have a purpose. [*Unhesitatingly.*] I in-
tend to become an emperor. [*He says the word simply,
unassumingly, and with complete candor.*]

THE FOUR. [*Astounded.*] What!

PEER. [*Nodding.*] Emperor. [*He looks at them, smiling.*]

THE FOUR. [*Uncertainly.*] Emperor over what? Where?

PEER. [*As before.*] Over the whole world.

BALLON. [*Excitedly.*] How, my friend?

PEER. A man can do anything with money. As a boy, I
rode high in my dreams on a horse in the clouds. And
usually I flopped down hard on my setter. But the purpose stood there fixed and certain. I've been true to myself and the rest has followed—true to my Gyntian self.

[*He stares at them, and for a moment the* FOUR *are
silent.*]

COTTON. [*Loudly, earnestly.*] But what then is this Gyntian self, sir?

PEER. [*Glibly, as he chuckles.*] What makes me me and not you—makes me different from you—[*Harshly.*] —you to take orders and me to give them. God is not the devil and the devil is not God. Simple. [*With a gesture similar to that of the old Troll Courtier in the former scene.*] You see the depth of it?

TRUMPETERSTRAALE. Now I glimpse what he's aiming at.

BALLON. [*Ecstatically.*] He's a sublime thinker.

EBERKOPF. [*Likewise.*] A mighty poet.

PEER. [*In glowing mood from the liquor.*] But this Gyntish self—I know what he is. He is an army of wishes, lusts, and appetites. He is an ocean of impulses, claims, and requirements. In short, he is everything that heaves and turmoils in my breast and makes me act and live as I do. [*Waving his umbrella in the air.*] But as the great Lord God of the Universe must have clay to make a world out of, so I also must have gold to make myself a king on earth.

BALLON. [*Now slyly.*] And you have gold—millions of it in your ship?

PEER. [*Pooh-poohing.*] Enough maybe for a little two-by-four king, but I must be a high and mighty king. I would be Gynt of all the globe—Emperor Gynt from top to toe. I must have more gold.

BALLON. [*Carried away.*] And you will possess the world's most exquisite women—

EBERKOPF. And all the hundred-year-old wine. [*He makes a sucking noise with his lips.*]

TRUMPETERSTRAALE. And the mightiest armies on earth.

COTTON. [*Holding up a warning hand.*] But how will you make this extra gold? You must have a profitable business opening.

PEER. That's the reason for our anchoring here by the Moroccan coast. The newspapers I received aboard informed me of important news. Tonight we set off northward. [*The* FOUR *half rise from their chairs, gazing out at* PEER *queryingly.*] God helps those who help themselves.

THE FOUR. [*In pleading unison.*] Tell us.

PEER. [*Barking the words out.*] Greece is in revolt.

[*The* FOUR YESMEN *leap fully up.*]

THE FOUR. What! The Greeks!

PEER. [*Turns off toward his hammock and sits down in it.*] There's an uprising.

THE FOUR. Hooray!

PEER. Turkey's in a turmoil.

BALLON. To Greece! The gate of glory stands open wide, and I'll help them with the sword of France.

EBERKOPF. And like the red Indians, I'll encourage them with war whoops—but at a distance. [*He waves his glass in the air and lets out a raucous cheer.*]

COTTON. And my friends and I, we'll help, too—by shipping war goods.

BALLON. [*Runs over to the hammock, grabs* PEER's *hand and kisses it.*] Your Excellency! Forgive me. I completely misjudged you.

[*The other* YESMEN *come crowding up.*]

EBERKOPF. [*Kissing* PEER's *hand likewise.*] I mistook you for a mere scoundrel.

COTTON. [*Taking* PEER's *other hand and kissing it.*] And I only for a fool.

TRUMPETERSTRAALE. [*Bending over and kissing* PEER *on the forehead.*] And please you, sir, I thought you were a riffraff Yankee sharper.

PEER. [*Made suspicious by their obsequiousness.*] Hanged if I understand you fellows.

COTTON. [*Quickly.*] We are overcome by your greatness, sir, by your Gyntish self—in all its Gyntish greatness. [*The* OTHERS *nod affirmingly.*] But when do we join the Greeks with ship and money?

PEER. [*Shaking his head and laughing.*] I fight on the strongest side. I lend my money to the Turks.

BALLON. Impossible!

EBERKOPF. You're joking!

PEER. [*Puffing on his cigar again.*] You four go to Greece. Fight for freedom and the right. Run, storm, make hell hot for the Turks. End your days in honor as a sacrifice for freedom. But as for me and my money—no thank you. [*Chuckling, he pulls the mosquito netting over himself and snuggles to sleep in his hammock.*]

[*The* ATTENDANT *strikes his lute again.*]

COTTON. [*Presently.*] Sleep and rest, sir. Sleep and rest, and we will watch.

PEER. Good old dogs—good dogs—

[*The scene now is filled with the somnolent oriental melody. The* FOUR YESMEN *look at one another and then down at the recumbent figure in the hammock. They turn back toward the table. The hammock dims down in shadow. The* FOUR MEN *gesture in pantomimic language to each other. They reach the table and begin to devour the remnants of food.*]

TRUMPETERSTRAALE. [*Softly.*] The swinish knave. Money, money!

[*They* ALL *fall silent in thought as the music plays. They chew on the remnants of food an instant.*]

BALLON. [*Suddenly, explosively.*] Damn, I felt myself so close to a turn of fortune.

EBERKOPF AND TRUMPETERSTRAALE. Aye, we did, we did.

[COTTON *indicates* PEER *in the hammock.*]

COTTON. The mighty Gynt is sleeping.

[*The* OTHERS *nod.*]

BALLON. [*Softly.*] And the ship is waiting.

EBERKOPF. With money in it.

TRUMPETERSTRAALE. Money from the poor Chinese— from the poor Negroes.

COTTON. And his emperor's dreams can end here in the sand.

EBERKOPF. The crew can be bought for a song.

COTTON. In the name of His Majesty, I requisition the yacht.

TRUMPETERSTRAALE. You what—?

COTTON. We pinch the whole caboodle.

BALLON. Quick, gentlemen, quick! [*They start stealing away toward the dinghy at the rear.*]

BALLON. [*Stopping.*] Still, it's a dirty trick. [*Shrugging his shoulders.*] But *enfin!*

[*The* MEN *hurry off and begin getting into the dinghy. And now the* FIRST ATTENDANT *runs to join them. He helps push the dinghy off.* COTTON *is standing up and the others are now sitting down in the boat.* COTTON *kisses his hand toward the sleeping* PEER.]

COTTON. Farewell, Emperor Gynt. Dream on. There's no bridge left to retreat over this time.

[*The dinghy with its crew of five now moves off around the curve in the shore. The light dies from the scene at the right and rear and comes up in an illumination on* PEER'S *sleeping figure. The* ATTENDANT *sitting on the sand continues his music for a while. And now the images and voices of* PEER'S *fermenting brain begin their animation in the air. The faint bird-cries and indistinct troll voices and vocables are heard at first. As they grow a little louder the* ATTENDANT *suddenly stops playing his lute. He springs up and runs after the deserting ones out at the left rear. The half-perceived medley of bird cries, troll voices, hymn singing and hallooings surge in louder and then fade down into a more stable and level volume of musical sound. The far-away drum in the earlier part of the play begins again. The light dims on* PEER'S *sleeping form and rises in a glow up on a stage-level behind and above him. Here like a mirage or vision in a dream appears* PEER'S *psychic haunting. The platform is crossed by a parapet. And higher up behind is a dais in front of a grey stone wall. Illumined on the wall behind the dais are the painted rays of a gleaming sun spread out from the throne-like chair all draped in scarlet silk. In the middle of the rays above the chair is a great poster-painting of* PEER GYNT, *the Emperor and Dictator, in life-like color.*

The figure of PEER *is seen standing behind the parapet—in front of the picture. He is wearing a black military uniform, his chest loaded with medals and orders, his shoulders blazing with scarlet epaulets. A gleaming scabbardless sword is at his belt.*

On either side of him are a number of grey uniformed HENCHMEN, *with long dark rifles held stiffly at their sides. They are facing toward the portrait, their backs to the audience. The drum beats louder. Far away the trumpets blare, and a mighty chorus of adulation from the throats of unseen thousands swells up from below.* PEER *steps forward and raises his hand in a small and careless salute. At the raising of his hand, the* HENCHMEN *turn around and step close to his side. Under the stiff grey military caps only flat black plates of steel show for faces. Their motions are blind, automaton, robot-like. The* TWO HENCHMEN *at the extreme right and left hold long opera glasses to their faces, peering watchfully down at the unseen crowd for possible assassins and spies. The others hold their long rifles at the ready, motionless as dummies.*]

VOICES. [*From below.*]
>   Vive l'Empereur!
>   Hail, Peer Gynt!
>   Heil! Heil!
>   The Emperor! The Emperor!
>   Peer Gynt! Peer Gynt!

[PEER'S *arm goes up in a terrific and long salute. The unseen people cheer madly. The trumpet blares again, and the light pours blindingly down on* PEER. *He stands there illumined in immortal power and pride. And now his invisible and myriad soldiers start marching by in review—on their way to conquer the world—the far-off rhythmic tramp of brutish hobnailed feet. Tatatata— tata! go the trumpets, and the snare drums rarara-ta! The marching feet come on—louder and louder still.*

Along in front of the parapet enters the TROLL BRAT, PEER'S *bastard son, carrying his little axe and limping in rhythm to the marching feet. Behind him walks the dark solemn figure of* SOLVEIG'S FATHER, *carrying a snow-white cross of Christ in one hand and a great open Bible on the palm of the other—illuminated in a dazzling light. The marching feet reach a crescendo of sound.* PEER *stands as if blinded and frozen in his stance of glory and strength. The* BRAT *lifts his little axe and takes dead aim at his father. He squints remorselessly along the helve, pulls the trigger, and the axe fires in a terrific explosion of flash and flame.* PEER *staggers and falls, shot through the heart. The* HENCHMEN *stare straight ahead, paying no attention to their fallen Emperor. The echoes of the explosion reverberate through the void, drowning out the marching feet and waking a pandemonium of bird cries, troll vocables, and ogre mumblings. The dream scene vanishes.*

The sleeping PEER *shrieks in his hammock. He bounds
to his feet and stands shivering and alone. The light
comes up on him, and the palm trees reappear. He looks
about him in waking dismay and horror. The light fills
the scene with a misty radiance from the moon high in
the sky. At the rear the yacht is moving with full steam
far out toward the open sea.* PEER *runs wildly up and
down. He spies the yacht and realizes what is happening.
He is thunderstruck.*]

PEER. [*A cry breaking from him.*] They are stealing
my gold. No—no—it's a dream. I'm asleep. [*Wringing his hands.*] A dream—it's got to be a dream. No—
it's the truth. They're putting to sea. [*Shaking his
fist.*] Scoundrels—thieves— [*Falling down on his
knees in an agony of pleading.*] God up there—Our
Father Who art in Heaven—listen—hear me. [*His
arms upraised.*] This is Peer Gynt—help me, Father
—help me, God! Back the engine—lower the gig—
[*Frenziedly pleading.*] Stop 'em, stop 'em—make something go wrong—hear me—hear me— [*Striking his
temple with his knuckles.*] Damn if he hears a thing—
He's deaf as usual when he's needed. A fine sort of
God you are. [*He stands and waves his hand at the sky.*]
I went out of the slave business. I sold my Negro planta-
tion. I sent missionaries to Asia. Well, Sir, one good
turn deserves another. Help me—help me— [*Out at sea
a stream of fire is seen shooting aloft from the yacht,
and the thick smoke slowly settles above it.* PEER *stands
petrified, and then a slow, roaring explosion comes rushing shoreward. He staggers under the impact and falls
down on the sand. The smoke drifts away. The ship
has disappeared.* PEER *begins talking to himself, gently,
softly, stricken in soul.*] Sunk. Gone to the bottom.

Everything—rats, men, all! [*A light breaking in his face.*] Praise be to God, I was not on it. I have escaped. [*With awed conviction.*] I was *meant* to be saved. They were meant to be destroyed. [*Raising his face now jubilantly.*] Thank you and bless you for saving me. You've kept an eye on me in spite of my sins. [*A great gust of breath goes out of him, and now there comes a faint, teasing rumble in the sky.*] What a wonderful thing to feel that Divine Providence specially protects you. [*He glances about him at the terrific and desolate waste.*] Protect, I say? [*He gets to his feet. A loud growl comes from the darkness. He jumps around terrified.*] What was that—a lion growling in the rushes— [*With chattering teeth.*] I am imagining things. Still it's all right to trust in God, but you better keep your powder dry. I'll find me a tree. And I'll sing a couple of hymns for good measure too if I can remember them. [*He tries to climb up one of the palm trees and fails. He gazes forlornly out to sea.*] Things don't look too promising, Peer Gynt. Anyway, he's got a fatherly feeling for me. I know that. [*He looks out to sea with a sigh.*] My ship and money gone to the bottom. He's not an economical God, that's a fact. Well, old Number One, you've got to be moving. [*He squares his shoulders, tightens his belt, picks up his umbrella from the table and resolutely starts hiking across the sand. The light begins to die, the medley of bird cries, troll voices and ogre mumblings comes surging in again and continues. The scene fades out.*]

PART TWO

Scene II

*The great desert. It is just before dawn. A
drowsy harmony of an Arab war song fills the
air. A group of warriors are camped off stage.
Presently a halloo is heard at the right. A*
SLAVE *runs across the scene at the rear, tearing his hair and beating his breast as he goes.*
ANOTHER SLAVE *comes running in to meet
him, tearing his clothes and wagging his head
in ululation likewise.*

FIRST SLAVE. The Emperor's white steed is stolen!

SECOND SLAVE. The Emperor's holy costume has been
taken!

OVERSEER. [*A brutal and powerful man in his oriental
garb, comes meeting them. He carries a whip in his
hand.*] I'll put a hundred lashes on the foot of every slave
—if you don't catch the thief.

[*He strikes at the* TWO SLAVES *with his whip and they
fly off at the right, the* OVERSEER *following them. The
flooding plop-plop of horses' hooves is heard as the warriors mount their horses nearby and go galloping off into
the desert. They continue their shouts and halloos as
they ride.*]

WARRIORS. Yay-ee—yay-ee! Hoa-hoa!

[*The light of the dawn grows in the east. Now the trotting feet of a single horse are heard approaching at the right front. The sound comes almost into the scene and stops. A moment passes. The shouting dies in the distance. A* THIEF *and a* HEELER *come in at the right front. They have evidently just dismounted. The* HEELER *holds to the end of a long bridle rein, and the* THIEF *carries a bundle in his arms.*]

THE THIEF. [*Looking off.*] The warriors' blades and lances are flashing and sparkling— [*Fearfully.*] The warriors are searching everywhere.

THE HEELER. Our heads will soon roll in the sand. Oh, oh.

THIEF. It is the will of Allah. [*Fatalistically.*] My father was a thief, so I must steal.

HEELER. [*Likewise.*] My father kept stolen goods, so must I.

THIEF. What is to be must be.

HEELER. We must be ourselves.

[*He reaches out and takes the bundle from the* THIEF, *sets it on the ground and opens it. A pile of gleaming jewels is disclosed as well as rich attire including a bejeweled coat and turban. The two of them squat down to enjoy their take.*]

THIEF. [*Listening.*] Somebody's coming.

HEELER. Hide the goods.

[*He flings the rein off to one side and clucking shoos the horse away and throws his crop down. The two*

swiftly roll up the bundle. The HEELER *finds a crevice
in the rock at the right front, crams the bundle in, and
the two of them go running off at the left front.* PEER
*presently comes in at the left rear, carrying the ruins of
his umbrella. He is a spectacle to look at—ragged and
unkempt. He is in bad shape physically and spiritually,
but he is trying manfully to measure up to his difficul-
ties. His words are more laconic and ironic than ever,
tinged even with a dour sense of humor.*]

PEER. [*Looking out toward the east and grimacing.*]
Another wonderful day. The air smells like fresh ma-
nure, and the beetle is already up rolling his ball of dung
in the dust. [*Peering off.*] And the morning, as the saying is, has gold in its mouth. [*He turns in toward the
rocks at the right and stops. He staggers a bit from
weakness and puts out his hand to steady himself.*]
The city man talks of getting away from it all. He
should come here. He could enjoy the silence of the
country. [*He comes over near where the jewels and
clothes are hidden. He gazes at the rock, which is now
bathed in the golden light of the rising sun.*] So still you
can hear yourself think. [*He scratches along the rocks
hunting for something to eat. He puts on his pince nez
with a foppish gesture and peers about him.*] Aha—a
petrified toad, looking at the world and seeing nothing.
[*Chuckling.*] Just being himself. [*He digs up an edible
root and chews on it, then contemplates the stem.*] I've
had meals that tasted better in my time. They say a man
must humble himself before he shall be exalted. [*Chuckling again.*] I'm humble enough all right. [*He pulls up
another root, chews on it and looks out over the desert.*]
I wonder what God intends to do with all this sand.
With proper machinery, a man might cut a canal, let

the water in from the ocean. Soon this whole white-hot
grave would grow green. Dew would drop from the sky
and the people would build cities. And factories would
be built. [*Firing up to his imagining.*] I could transplant
the whole Norwegian race here from their cold climate.
I could build a capital and call it Peeropolis. And the
country would be named Gyntianna. [*Excitedly.*] Only
money is needed to do it. Gold is the key. A new crusade
against death! Gold—gold! [*In his growing fervor and
excitement he pulls at a large plant growing in the rocks.*]
Aye, I will send out the call of freedom over the world
to bring the people to my kingdom. [*Echoingly.*] Kingdom? Half my kingdom for a horse! [*A horse whinnies
close by at the right. He jumps back and in doing so
jerks the plant up by the roots. A rock is dislodged and
falls down. And there the great bundle of jewels spills
open before him. He looks at them an instant incredulously and then glances up at the sky as if to acknowledge
to whatever Power resides there that he,* PEER GYNT,
*recognizes its beneficence. He salutes the sky with his
hand.*] These gifts from heaven I acknowledge—a horse!
and clothing! and jewels! [*The sky rumbles in jocose
answer.* PEER *examines the jewels, fills his pockets, and
then frenziedly begins putting on the rich coat and turban.*] They're the real thing. It's a miracle! They say
faith can move mountains. But what about bringing a
horse to pass in the middle of the desert? [*He reaches
out his hand and clucks to the unseen horse. At this instant there sounds as if from a minaret in the sky the
muezzin's call to morning prayer.* PEER *looks about him
astounded. The call is repeated. The laughter of* GIRLS *is
heard tinkling in the air around him.*] And not only a
horse, but girls. Jehovah improves.

GIRLS' VOICES. [*Chanting nearby.*]
The prophet has come,
The prophet has come,
The prophet, the master,
The everything-knowing,
To us, to us he has come!

[ANITRA *and a flock of* GIRLS *come dancing into the scene, followed by a few musicians, playing a flute, a lute, a drum, and tambourines. Several* ATTENDANTS *push forward huge and swollen pillows and then retire. A great roll of silk tent covering comes billowing down and hangs shelteringly in the air, and the* GIRLS *push* PEER *onto a divan of pillows. A long smoking pipe is put into his hand. Bewildered but ready for anything, he enters into the play of wiles and beauty.*]

GIRLS. [*Chanting in time to the music.*]
Over the sand he came riding,
The prophet, the master,
The never-failing.
To us, to us he has come—
Through the sand sea sailing.
Stir the flute and beat the drum—
Prophet, the prophet has come.

[ANITRA, *the buxom lithesome young woman leader, springs out in front of the dancers and begins her exquisite motions in front of* PEER. *Her eyes are dark and lovely and her teeth pearly. Through her red lips the rhythmic words babble in joyous delight.*]

ANITRA. His charger is white as the milk is
Streaming in rivers through paradise.
Bend your knees! Bow your heads!

[*The* DANCING GIRLS *bow their heads and move backward into the shadows, keeping a rhythmic and concerted
body motion there as accompaniment to* ANITRA'S *ex-
hibition.*]

His eyes are like stars gleaming and gentle,
Gold and pearls spring forth on his breast.
He the wonderful one has come!
Through the eastern world he came
Like an earth son bejeweled.

CHORUS OF GIRLS. [*In unison as they dance.*]
Stir the flute and beat the drum.
The prophet, the prophet has come!

[*The music swells out and then is muted down as the
dance continues.*]

PEER. [*Jovially.*] So they take me for a prophet. Well,
that suits me, though I have no intention to commit
fraud. [*The dance has continued. The* GIRLS *led by*
ANITRA *wreathe themselves around and behind* PEER
as he chants his crowing statement further.] It's a per-
sonal matter, anyway. I can go as I came. My horse
stands ready. In short, I've got the situation well in hand.
So dance away, children of nature. The prophet is enjoying himself. His belly's empty, but his eyes are satisfied.

ANITRA. [*Caressingly.*] Master, Anitra has come to thee.

PEER. What does my slave Anitra want?

ANITRA. [*Regarding him.*] To serve you.

THE GIRLS. [*Chanting from the shadows.*]
The prophet is good, the prophet is sad

For the evil which the sons of the dust have done.
The prophet is mild, praise be his mildness.
To sinners he opens up paradise. .

[ANITRA *is now working her seductiveness on* PEER. *He watches her somewhat cynically, yet intrigued.*]

PEER. You're a delicious piece, all right. But you might say some of your contours are a little extravagant. After all, beauty is a convention. But your feet are not clean, that's certain—nor your arms, either. [*Calling.*] Anitra.

ANITRA. Your slave has heard.

PEER. The prophet is touched—he is tempted. He will make you an angel in paradise.

ANITRA. Impossible, Master. [*She leans out by him and puts her head against him.*]

PEER. I really mean it.

ANITRA. But I have no soul.

PEER. Then you can get one.

ANITRA. How, Master?

PEER. Come here. Let me measure your—er—intelligence. [*He pulls her close and appraises her figure.*]

ANITRA. [*Demurely.*] The prophet is good—but I would prefer—

PEER. Speak up, my daughter, don't be bashful.

ANITRA. I don't care about a soul. Give me— [*Giggling.*]—that beautiful opal.

PEER. [*Pulls a jewel out of his turban and hands it to her.*] You're a natural daughter of Eve all right. And

I am a natural son of Adam. [*He catches her face in his hands and kisses her. Then in a scramble of pleasure he picks up the lute left by the musicians and begins to sing, accompanying himself.*]

> He barred the door of paradise
> And took the key along.
> The nórth wind bore him out to sea
> While lovely women all forlorn
> Wept on the ocean strand.
>
> I climbed aboard my desert ship,
> A bark on four stout legs.
> It foamed beneath the lashing whip—
> Oh, catch me for a flitting bird
> I'll trill upon the bough.

[ANITRA *has laid her head in his lap. He strums the lute and bends over her.*]

PEER. Sighs of love— No, by golly, she's snoring. [*He strikes the lute again and stares down at her.*] Well, her sleeping shows she believes in my self-control. A cup so sweet, and not tasting a drop!

ANITRA. [*Dreamily, murmurously.*] Master, dost thou call me in the night?

PEER. Your master calls. [*He lifts up her head and kisses her again.*]

ANITRA. Master, is that the way you can give me a soul?

PEER. That's one way of doing it. A little gift helps too, say a jewelled ring around your ankle. [*He fastens a jewel around her ankle and feels her leg. She kicks, lies back, and begins to snore again.*] My lady sleeps and snores. She's overcome by my eloquence no doubt. [*He lifts her head gently aside, propping her on a pillow and gazes down at her with a touch of sardonic humor. He pulls handfuls of jewels out of his pocket and drops them in her lap. He pulls off his jewelled coat and kneels a little rheumatically by her to spread it over her.*] Here are trinkets, Anitra. So does a man persuade a woman who persuades him.

[*He lies down and pulls her to him under the coat. She springs away and fights at him.*]

ANITRA. I'll bite you.

PEER. You little rascal.

ANITRA. Be ashamed. An old prophet like you!

PEER. Your prophet's not old.

ANITRA. Let me go. [*She breaks free, and with her eye on him quickly gathers up the jewels and trinkets.*] Are you a true prophet?

PEER. Look how the little woodpecker tosses her head!

[*He smiles at her.*]

ANITRA. Give me that ring from your finger.

PEER. Take it, sweet Anitra. Take them all. [*He hands her the remaining jewels from his pockets. She stuffs them in her clothes and gathers up the others which have spilled on the ground. She looks at him and then reaches out and strokes his face.*] It's a heavenly feeling, Anitra, to be loved so unselfishly. [ANITRA *picks up the* HEELER'S *riding crop from the ground.*] It makes me young again.

ANITRA. Have you any more rings?

PEER. Here, catch. [*He throws her the last of his jewels.*]
I can leap like that buck on Gendin Ridge. Hey, I will
dance for you. [*He dances and sings.*]

> I am a happy rooster.
> Peck me, my little chick.
> Hey hop! Let me dance.
> I am a happy rooster.

[*He puts his hand to his back suddenly. A stitch has
caught him.* ANITRA *bursts into mocking laughter.*]

ANITRA. You are sweating, Prophet! Let me have that
heavy thing at your belt.

PEER. What a loving heart you've got! [*He unfastens a
heavy purse and throws it to her and then goes on dancing.*]

ANITRA. [*Counting her money.*] It's a beautiful thing
to see a prophet dancing.

PEER. It is a beautiful thing to dance for love—to suffer
for love. [*He drops down on his knees by her.*]

ANITRA. [*Fondling her riches and leaning toward him.*]
You like to suffer for love?

PEER. Yes, death and damnation. Let me suffer, a sharp
and violent pain—a spasm.

[*The horse off scene neighs.* ANITRA *listens.*]

ANITRA. Anitra obeys the prophet—

[*She picks up the riding crop from the ground, strikes
PEER suddenly in the face, blinding him. He falls backward with a howl of pain. She runs off at the left front,
the horse is heard neighing again. Immediately after-*

*ward we hear the flooding sound of hooves scudding
away as* ANITRA *rides off.* PEER *holds his face in his
hands.*

PEER. [*Crying out.*] The damned b—b—tch! [*He staggers to his feet and rubs his arm across his bruised face.
He snarls grimly and sardonically to himself, wags his
head and stares off in the direction* ANITRA *has ridden.
He listens to the fading hoofbeats. Slowly he begins pulling off his fine Turkish clothing, piece by piece. He takes
his little travelling cap out of his coat pocket, puts it
on and stands again in his raggle-taggle European dress.
He throws the turban far away from him with a mut-
tered oath.*] So there is the Turk and here is me. This
heathenish stuff is no damned good! Lucky I can get rid
of the prophet by getting rid of his clothes. [*He takes a
few steps limpingly and uncertainly forward.*] That
hussy came within an ace of making a fool out of me.
[*Shaking his head.*] What in the devil made me act so
crazy! [*Chuckling.*] Only a fool can be a prophet.
[*Hitching up his belt.*] And women—I say to hell with
all of 'em.

[*He takes a step forward, then lifts his foot as if it
pinches him. He pulls his old jacket about him, sits down
on the ground and begins to work at his bedraggled shoe,
getting the sand out of it. The faint notes of a flute are
heard, beginning far away and as if high up in the air.
They come a little nearer, reminiscent of Norway and
the opening melody of the play. A misty light grows at
the back. The billowing roll of silk has disappeared. Now
up in the air behind* PEER *in the distance we see the figure
of* SOLVEIG *set as in a weather halo. She is a middle-aged
woman now yet still fair and beautiful. She is sitting at*

a wheel and spinning. We hear her voice singing though her lips are motionless, her melodic thoughts going out to the wastrel across the void.]

SOLVEIG'S VOICE.

The winter will come and spring go by,
The summer and long autumn too.
But someday you'll come—I know you will come
And I'll wait for you as I said I would.

[*In the vision a goat is seen coming up to her. It lays its bearded head on her knee. She strokes it and goes on singing.* PEER *sits as if transfixed.*]

May God give you joy wherever you go.
May God keep you safe in his care.
Here will I wait till you come back to me.
And if you don't come, then in heaven I'll wait.

[PEER *springs to his feet, turns and runs frantically toward the vision. But it has disappeared. He spins helplessly about. His voice chokes in his throat. He stands bent and broken. The light is coming full now from the east, and there at the back another creature has appeared. It is the Sphinx and it looks much like the Cheshire Cat in "Alice in Wonderland"—with its face and paws projecting in front of its body.* PEER *now ties his shoe and moves forward as if on his long journey. He sees the Sphinx and starts back with a cry. Then he moves curiously forward studying the silent figure.*]

PEER. I've seen that creature somewhere before. Where was it?—Was it in the north? Or in the south? [*He stares at the Sphinx.*] I remember now. It was that damned ogre I met in the darkness. [*Pondering.*] The

fellow that said "Go round about." Or did I dream it?
[*He takes a few steps in the direction of the Sphinx.*]
I guess you are the same fellow, Mr. Ogre, though in the
daylight you look different—like a lion. You wouldn't
answer me that night in the dark. Answer me now.
[*Shouting toward the Sphinx.*] Hey, Ogre, who are
you?

[*His voice echoes across the desert as in the Norway
mountains of his youth—"Who are you, who are you?"*]

A VOICE. [*Behind the Sphinx.*] *Ach! Sfinx. Wer bist du?*

PEER. *Wer bist du?* The thing speaks German.

THE VOICE. *Wer bist du?*

BEGRIFFENFELDT. [*Comes out from behind the Sphinx.
He is a stout German, dressed in dark clothes with a
bowler hat and heavy-lensed glasses. His face is clean
shaven except for a thick blond brush of moustache.
Bowing.*] Dr. Begriffenfeldt at your service.

PEER. What are you doing here?

BEGRIFFENFELDT. I am studying the riddle of personal-
ity. [*Bowing again.*] And you, sir?

PEER. I am calling on an old friend.

BEGRIFFENFELDT. The Sfinx.

PEER. I knew him in the old days. [*Suddenly shouting.*]
Who are you?

[BEGRIFFENFELDT *jerks up his head and stares at him.*
PEER'S *words echo away—"Who are you?"*]

BEGRIFFENFELDT. "Who are you?" Exactly my query.

[*He suddenly shakes hands with* PEER.] You know him, man? Speak. Can you tell me what he is?

PEER. What he is? Yes, that's easy enough. [*Walking about and then turning sharply on* BEGRIFFENFELDT. He is himself.

BEGRIFFENFELDT. [*Is astounded and leaps high in the air with a whicker of joy.*] Ha! The riddle of this creature shines before me like a light. You are certain he is— himself?

PEER. [*Cups his ear and leans toward the Sphinx listening. Satisfied.*] That's what he says. [*He slaps himself in a whiff of satirical fun.*]

BEGRIFFENFELDT. Himself. True, true. Simplicity itself. [*Admiringly.*] The wise men before you could not solve it. [*Removing his hat.*] Your name, *mein herr?*

PEER. Peer Gynt.

BEGRIFFENFELDT. Peer Gynt! Allegorical. [*Repeating, savoringly.*] Peer Gynt—that is to say, the unknown one, the coming one—who was foretold to me. [*He taps the center of his skull with a big forefinger.*]

PEER. Foretold to you?

BEGRIFFENFELDT. Bestimnt. And here I am to meet you. What a night of waiting! My forehead hammers and cracks. [*Stopping and staring at* PEER.] What are you?

PEER. [*With a modest smirk.*] I have always tried to be—like that fellow there—myself. And besides, here is my passport to prove it. [*He indicates his tattered garments.*]

BEGRIFFENFELDT. [*With a shout.*] We have found our king! Our king has come!

PEER. King?

BEGRIFFENFELDT. Our true emperor. [*He grabs* PEER'S *hand and starts pulling him along.*] Our Emperor on the basis of self.

PEER. Hey, hold on a minute!

BEGRIFFENFELDT. The statesmen have assembled. They are waiting your wisdom.

[*He starts leading* PEER *away at the left rear. The scene fades out. In the distance the melody of* SOLVEIG'S *song rises wordlessly and continues.*]

PART TWO

Scene III

The great courtyard of an insane asylum in Cairo, with high walls around. In the center at the back is a huge steel black globe representative of the world, with white markings of the continents showing on it. A big door with iron vertical bars is in the center of it. When the light comes up on the scene, two uniformed GUARDS *are standing at the left and right, and the globe is in shadow. They are dressed somewhat like modern male nurses in a mental hospital. The door at the right front opens and* BEGRIFFENFELDT *leads* PEER GYNT *in. A chatter sets up from the inmates within the globe, and the two* GUARDS *turn and salute* BEGRIFFENFELDT *who locks the door behind him and puts the key in his pocket.* PEER GYNT *is in good humor and is just finishing the last of a roll and a piece of sausage which have been provided him somewhere on the way.*

PEER. What amazing learning, sir! I can't make heads or tails of a thing you say. [*He looks about him.*] So this is the statesmen's club, eh?

TWO GUARDS. [*In unison.*] Good morning, Herr Direktor.

BEGRIFFENFELDT. [*Acknowledges their greetings with a careless gesture.*] Here you will find every point of view of the nations represented. Even the backward people have their say. [*Calling suddenly and angrily.*] Into the cage with you guards at once.

THE GUARDS. [*Astounded.*] But we are the guards!

BEGRIFFENFELDT. Get going, get going! Things are changing in the world today and we've got to change with them. [*He bounds over to the great ball of the world, jerks open the iron door and gestures them in. We see a number of white faces and resplendent diplomatic figures inside the ball.* BEGRIFFENFELDT *greets them with his great announcement.*] Ladies and gentlemen, the Emperor Peer Gynt has arrived this morning. You can figure the meaning of that out for yourselves, I say no more.

[*He slams the door shut and the disappointed chatter of the* INMATES *goes up.*]

PEER. But Herr Doktor, you've got me wrong.

BEGRIFFENFELDT. Mr. Peer Gynt, can you keep a secret? I must speak out, my heart is full.

PEER. [*Glancing about him apprehensively.*] What is it?

BEGRIFFENFELDT. Promise me you won't faint.

PEER. All right.

BEGRIFFENFELDT. [*Grabs him fiercely by the arms and leans toward him. In solemn announcement.*] Common sense passed away in death this morning at eleven o'clock— [*He points a long and piercing finger toward* PEER.] The hour I met you by the Sphinx.

PEER. [*With a shout.*] God help me! He's crazy!

BEGRIFFENFELDT. [*Wagging his head.*] A very deplorable thing. Reason is dead. And in my position, sir, you see it is doubly deplorable. [*He touches his forehead in a salute to himself.*] For this institution has always stood for an insane asylum.

PEER. Asylum!

BEGRIFFENFELDT. Not any longer—since the world has gone crazy.

PEER. [*Pale, mopping his forehead with his sleeve.*] Now I understand this place. [*Jerking up his head and gazing off.*] And this man is mad—and no one knows it.

[*He pulls himself loose from* BEGRIFFENFELDT *and steps over to one side.*]

BEGRIFFENFELDT. [*Shaking his head.*] The world is mad! Reason takes refuge here—with you as emperor.

PEER. [*Throwing up his hands.*] Crazy—completely crazy.

BEGRIFFENFELDT. Completely sane. Long live sanity! [*He rushes over to the iron door to the globe and jerks it open, calling loudly.*] Come out, come out! The time that shall be has arrived. We now proclaim it! Long live Peer Gynt!

[*A raucous howl and cheer come out of the cage. The* INMATES *now enter the scene from the cage, blinking as if their eyes were disturbed by the sudden light. These are the creatures who inhabit the world and do its business. They represent something of a cross-section of the nations—a Hindu, a Chinese, an American, an English-*

*man, a Japanese, Russian, Negro, etc. They are dressed
as diplomats and statesmen, some generals, an admiral or
two, a few capitalists, two feminine socialites, beautifully
dressed and lorgnetted and big-bosomed, and some
square-set and power-muscled workmen—each in his
native costume.* BEGRIFFENFELDT, *the director, steps in
front of them like a circus master before his pets. The
inmates line up in front of him, some bowing, curtseying
and saluting, each according to his calling and the
method of his country.*]

BEGRIFFENFELDT. [*Addressing them.*] Freedom's dawn
has arrived. Greet your new emperor.

[*The* INMATES *gaze at* PEER *with chilly eyes.*]

PEER. [*Protesting.*] But the honor's so great, so beyond
all reason—

BEGRIFFENFELDT. Now is no time for false modesty, your
Highness.

[*The* INMATES *applaud suddenly.*]

PEER. [*Shaking his head.*] Damned if I'm fit for the job.
I'm too stupid.

BEGRIFFENFELDT. A man who is himself in all circum-
stances!—the hour calls for him and the occasion de-
mands.

[*He gestures around him, the* INMATES *applaud again.*]

PEER. To be one's self is all right. But here I understand
it seems that everybody is not himself—he is out of himself, as it were—crazy, you know.

BEGRIFFENFELDT. Here one is one's self with a venge-
ance. He is one's self here and not a bit of anything

else—here each tub stands on its own bottom. To use your words, mighty sir—each man is thinking only of Number One. [PEER *stares at the* INMATES *in perplexity. For each one now has put his arms up crossed in front of his eyes as if cutting off his sight and communing with himself.* BEGRIFFENFELDT *goes on.*] Each one is closed up in himself with the bung of self. We are ourselves here, in thought and in deed. [*The* INMATES *drop their hands and nod their heads jubilantly.*] It's clear as crystal that you are the very man for the throne.

PEER. It's a job fit only for the devil himself.

BEGRIFFENFELDT. Don't be discouraged. [*Frantically.*] Don't deny us, sir. Everything is somewhat new in the beginning. You will get used to it. I will introduce you. [*The* INMATES *have started moving back and forth in the scene as if taking their morning exercise. The director looks at them pleasantly. He studies them.*] I choose one at random—one of the best. Since reason has died in the world—he conforms no less to reason. [*He indicates a* NEGRO WORKMAN *who carries a mummy on his back, a short squatty effigy with the dry dead face of an aristocrat. The effigy wears a peaked headdress, with a gleaming cross standing up behind. This creature of nationalism and prejudice and pride resembles a member of the Ku-Klux-Klan. The* WORKMAN *wears a cap and overalls and a sleeveless grimy shirt. At a gesture from* BEGRIFFENFELDT *he trots out eagerly with his mummy and bows low in front of* PEER. BEGRIFFENFELDT *addresses him.*] Please declare to our new emperor how matters stand with you, my good man.

WORKMAN. I carry a blue-blood on my back. His ancestors go back to Pharaoh. He has fought wars with

the Turks both right and left and has whipped them to
a frazzle. The people have praised him as a God and
built temples to him. [*Furiously.*] Temples to him! To
him! [*He strikes his breast.*] I want them to build temples to me—a working man. My folks are old as Adam.
[*Holding out his hands.*] Toil and sweat and calloused
hands. The question is how to become a king like this
fellow.

PEER. And ride on people's backs?

WORKMAN. [*Hopping up and down.*] Oh! Oh! Oh!
[*Pleadingly.*] You must know how to make me equal
to him. Our emperor must know these things.

PEER. [*After examining his hands.*] Your case is hope-
less.

[*The* WORKMAN *stares at him.*]

BEGRIFFENFELDT. [*Harshly.*] You better go hang yourself.

WORKMAN. Oh, oh, oh! [*With a cry.*] I'll do it! [*Calling around him.*] Who's got a rope? It will hurt a little
at first, but soon I won't feel a thing.

[*He hurries back toward the group. A* CARPENTER *meets
him carrying a rope looped in a noose in one hand and a
saw in the other. The* WORKMAN *throws the rope over
a convenient beam and prepares to hang himself.*]

BEGRIFFENFELDT. See how obedient he is to orders.

PEER. [*With a cry.*] But for God's sake man, look! He's
really hanging himself. I'm getting sick— Excuse me.
I'll be going.

BEGRIFFENFELDT. [*Holding him.*] You can't leave like this—suddenly resign the throne. It simply isn't done. [*As* PEER *persists.*] Are you mad, your Highness?

PEER. Not mad yet. But if I stay here I will be.

[*The* INMATES *begin to chatter and squeal. They part into two groups and look toward the rear. The minister* HUSSEIN *forces himself in through the crowd. He is dressed like a diplomat but in the semblance of a writing pen. His top hat is cut back and upward resembling the stub point of the pen. His coat is closefitting and swallow-tailed and his pin-striped trousers are straight-creased and long. He carries a portfolio under his arm and a cane. He looks eagerly about him.*]

HUSSEIN. I hear the emperor has arrived. [*He lifts his pince-nez and peers forward.* PEER *puts on his pince-nez and gazes back at him.*] It's you!

PEER. [*Desperately.*] The will of the people.

HUSSEIN. The world problems have piled up pending your arrival. [*He pulls out a sheaf of diplomatic correspondence from his portfolio.*]

PEER. [*Tearing his hair.*] Crazier and crazier.

HUSSEIN. [*Bowing deeply.*] I am a writing pen. I write what you bid me to.

PEER. [*Tearing open his old shirt.*] And I'm a white sheet of paper to write on then.

HUSSEIN. [*Panting.*] Paper! Paper! [*Piteously.*] Somebody tell me what to write! What is the message? I'm too dull to write—I must get myself sharpened. [*Pointing his cane at* PEER.] Sharpen me, and quick. The hour

grows late. The sun is going down. Freedom is per-
ishing.

PEER. [*Sneering.*] Let it perish—so what?

HUSSEIN. Sharpen me, sharpen me! I must write!

BEGRIFFENFELDT. [*Whips out a gleaming knife from his
pocket.*] The knife. Sharpen yourself.

HUSSEIN. [*Grabs it.*] I must sharpen myself.

[*He cuts his throat. The* INMATES *applaud. He staggers.*]

BEGRIFFENFELDT. Don't splatter us with your blood,
please.

PEER. [*Wildly.*] Hold him!

HUSSEIN. Don't forget the postscript. I lived and died
without coming to the point. [*Sobbing.*] I only wrote
what they told me to.

[*He collapses and the two* CLERKS *drag him away into
the shadows at the rear.*

PEER. [*Half-fainting, calling up to the sky.*] Emperor in
heaven—or somewhere—the guardian of all the fools on
earth—maybe. Whoever you are, help me! Help me!

[*He flings up his hands supplicatingly, spins around and
falls fainting on the ground. A sort of dwarfish* COURT
FOOL *comes forward toward* BEGRIFFENFELDT *with a
straw wreath in his hand.* BEGRIFFENFELDT *takes it and
with a leap sits astride* PEER. *The* INMATES *crowd forward and look down at their recumbent King.*]

BEGRIFFENFELDT. The divine afflatus has seized our Em-

peror. Like the oracle he will soon prophesy to us. Crown
him.

VOICES. [*Ad lib.*] Crown him! Crown our Emperor.

[*Several of the* INMATES *rush forward and help lift*
PEER *up on limber feet. They push the wreath of straw
down on his brow.*]

BEGRIFFENFELDT. Long live the Emperor of the Self!

VOICES. [*In a wild cry.*] Long live the great Peer Gynt!

[*The* INMATES *applaud and cheer and several of them
start a skipping dance around* PEER *like children around
a Maypole. The* BUTTONMOLDER *in the guise of the
Stranger comes strolling in at the right front.* BEGRIF-
FENFELDT *sees him.*]

BEGRIFFENFELDT. [*Fearfully.*] Eek!

[*The others see the dark figure and start back in horror.
As they turn,* PEER *staggers and would fall but for the*
BUTTONMOLDER *who hurries forward, catches him and
steadies him. The* INMATES *now flee back into their cage.
For a moment* BEGRIFFENFELDT *remains behind, then
he too backs away as the* BUTTONMOLDER *holds out his
casting ladle, using it as if it were a magic wand to put
a spell over the place. The light now fades out at the back
and the ball of the world disappears in darkness. Only*
PEER *and his visitor are seen at the left front, illuminated
in a circle of light—the darkness all around them. Psy-
chologically for the audience it is as though the scene had
changed. The* BUTTONMOLDER *gazes straight at* PEER,
as he holds him up. The raging and muttering of the IN-
MATES *in the cage die out.*]

BUTTONMOLDER. Your old acquaintance, Peer Gynt.

PEER. I don't know you.

BUTTONMOLDER. I know you well enough. I've followed you about the world from time to time. You need me now.

PEER. [*Frightened.*] Get away from me.

BUTTONMOLDER. [*Ingratiatingly.*] When a fellow is standing with one foot in the grave—he shouldn't say that.

PEER. [*Grabbing his empty pocket.*] If it's money you want—

BUTTONMOLDER. The same old Peer—trying to buy his way to salvation. I don't want your money. [*Bluntly.*] I want your honorable corpse.

PEER. [*In horror.*] Corpse!

BUTTONMOLDER. It would be used for a scientific purpose.

PEER. [*Loudly.*] Turn me loose!

BUTTONMOLDER. But my dear fellow, consider. It would be a great advantage to *you*. I'd have you thoroughly examined—have you opened up to the daylight by the surgeon's knife.

PEER. Help! Help!

BUTTONMOLDER. Don't get excited—only a mere corpse.

PEER. [*Moaning.*] Oh, oh!

BUTTONMOLDER. [*Chuckles.*] You're a funny fellow, Peer Gynt. You turn white as a sheet when somebody talks about touching your precious body. But what about

your soul? That's what I really want—your soul—the
seat of dreams. [*Holding out his ladle and opening it.*]
I see my diagnosis was correct from the beginning. You
must go back the way you came. Be melted down.

PEER. Die? [*Gasping.*] Leave me, you scarecrow. Beat
it! I'm not going to die.

BUTTONMOLDER. You might as well. You haven't proved
your point.

PEER. What point?

BUTTONMOLDER. Your right to go on living. [*Shaking
his head.*] A man can't find a thing by running away
from it. That's what you've been doing all your life—
running away.

PEER. [*Angrily.*] You're one of these smart Alecks—
know everything.

BUTTONMOLDER. I know when it's time to go home.

PEER. I happen to be here in this—madhouse. This is my
home for the moment.

BUTTONMOLDER. I see you're still a hard-headed fellow.
But time will soften it. I will be waiting, Peer. We will
meet again. [*He glides away into the shadow at the right
front.*]

PEER. [*Gazes after him.*] He was one of these mealy-
mouthed Puritans after all. [*Echoing.*] Time will soften
it. [*He falls to sudden brooding, muttering to himself.*]
The trouble with me is I've always been too soft, too
goodhearted. If I had my life to live over I'd change my
tune all right. I'd see what getting tough would do.
I'd be tough. [*Echoingly again.*] Time to go home.

[*Straightening up and striking his palms together.*]
That's right. I might get the old farm back—somehow
I might, by fair means or foul. [*Jubilantly, slightly hys-
terical.*] And I'd rebuild the old house the way I planned
—bright as a palace it would be. And the people would
come and look at it and say, "Peer Gynt's come back on
top of the world."

[*He takes a step or two in his new resolve, sees the straw
crown, picks it up and throws it from him toward the
cage door in the darkness. The* INMATES *there mutter
and growl at him. He shrinks back.* BEGRIFFENFELDT
*comes out of the shadows, picks up the straw crown and
holds it aloft.*]

BEGRIFFENFELDT. [*In a loud cry.*] Long live the Emperor Peer Gynt!

INMATES. [*In the darkness cheer. Repeating the cry.*]
Long live the Emperor!

[PEER *turns suddenly and runs away at the left front,
his face lifted in determination down the long road that
leads back to Norway.* BEGRIFFENFELDT, *forlorn, bows
twice to the audience in the theatre, steps back into the
cage with the crown and slams the door behind him. The
raucous growling and chattering of the* INMATES *rises
and continues as the light fades out.*]

PART TWO

Scene IV

A little churchyard high in the mountains of Norway. A funeral is underway in the rear of the scene. The young people in the earlier part of the play are now the elderly people in this scene with sons and daughters of their own. In the foreground we recognize INGRID *dressed in black widow's weeds. Standing with her is the* MINISTER, SOLVEIG'S *father, now an ancient man with flowing white beard. And somewhat off to one side* ASLAK, *the smith, with his aged wife, the* DARKEYED GIRL *in Scene 2 of Act 1.* ASLAK *is bowed on his stick. Several* YOUNG GIRLS *are standing by the grave with flower wreaths in their hands. When the light comes up the* PEOPLE *are singing in rich harmony, their hymn books held before them.*

PEOPLE. [*Led by the* MINISTER.]
　　What shall I, frail man, be pleading?
　　Who for me be interceding,
　　When the just are mercy needing?

　　King of majesty tremendous,
　　Who dost free salvation send us
　　Fount of pity, then befriend us!

127

MINISTER. Blessed is the man that walketh not in the counsel of the ungodly. He shall be like a tree planted by the rivers of water. His leaf shall not wither and whatsoever he doeth shall prosper.

PEOPLE. [*Reciting in unison.*] The ungodly are not so, but are like the chaff which the wind driveth away.

MINISTER. For the Lord knoweth the way of the righteous. But the way of the ungodly shall perish.

PEOPLE. [*In unison as before.*] And there is no darkness nor the shadow of death where the workers of iniquity may hide themselves.

MINISTER. Blessed be the name of the Lord.

PEOPLE. Blessed be the name of the Lord.

[*At a gesture from the old* MINISTER, *the* YOUNG GIRLS *begin laying their flowers on the grave. The* PEOPLE *lift their hymn books again and continue singing while the flowers are put down.*]

PEOPLE. [*Led by the* MINISTER.]
    Think, good Jesus, my salvation
    Cost thy wondrous incarnation!
    Leave me not to reprobation!

    Faint and weary, thou has sought me,
    On the cross of suffering bought me
    Shall such grace be vainly brought me?

MINISTER. [*As the* YOUNG GIRLS *finish placing the flowers.*] Now the soul of our departed brother goes to its judgement on high and the body remains an empty husk behind. Thus in the gate of death man's faith has raised

the symbol of eternal life. [*Looking down at the grave.*]
Mads Moen was not rich and he was not brilliant. His
voice was weak, his bearing was humble. [PEER *enters
from the right. He has aged since we saw him last—on
his long return home. His beard is scraggly and wind-
blown and he is leaning on a heavy gnarled peasant's
stick. He draws up nearer to the group listening. The*
MINISTER *continues.*] He was no leading citizen it is
true. His life was quiet. In the narrowness of his family
he found the work he was to do. He did it to the best of
his ability. And he was great because he was himself—
himself in terms of his duty. His word was his bond and
his character was the trust of honest men. [*Standing
closer to the grave he picks up some dirt and lets it
trickle downward.*] And therefore peace be with you,
you quiet fighter.

PEER. [*Sardonically, as he turns away.*] A very edifying
sermon. [*Chuckling.*] "Himself in terms of his duty."
A poor way of life I'd say—in fact, a kind of slavery.

MINISTER. [*Putting his hand comfortingly on* INGRID'S
shoulder.] Sister Ingrid, dry your tears. Your husband
is not dead. Mads Moen lives in the heart of his friends.

PEER. Mads Moen!

MINISTER. This is the true immortality. He who lives
within our hearts cannot die. His good deeds blossom
like flowers in our remembrance.

[INGRID *stands there wiping the tears from her eyes with
a showy white handkerchief.* PEER *stares at the gathering. The* MINISTER *lifts his hand again and the song resumes.*]

PEOPLE. [*Led by the* MINISTER.]
    Wordless are my prayers and sighing.
    Yet good Lord in grace complying,
    Rescue me from fires undying.

[*The* MINISTER *turns and leads the procession of mourn-
ers away at the right rear, all singing as they go.*]

    While the wicked are confounded,
    Doomed to flames of woe unbounded,
    Call me with thy saints surrounded.

[*They go on away at the right rear singing, their words
fading down in the distance.* PEER *stands a moment as if
caught in thought, then shrugging his shoulders he
moves over among the graves and stands looking down
at the flowers. He pokes a wreath carelessly with the
point of his stick.*]

PEER. The church remains the true comforter still—for
the hoi polloi. [*Shaking his head.*] But what the hell
good is it to tell a dead man—he reaps what he sows!
[*He stands musing at the headstone.*] Well, Mads Moen,
you still live in the hearts of your friends. But it looks
to me like you're dead and buried—soon to be set upon
by the waiting worm.] *Some of the* YOUNGER PEOPLE *at-
tracted by* PEER'S *behavior and wild appearance hang
about in the rear looking at him.* ASLAK *re-enters,
prompted by his usual curiosity.*] Go around, said the
Voice. Well, this proves him wrong. Death's a gate all
have to pass through.

[*He sits down on the headstone and puts his chin on the
nub of his cudgel. Other people have come in. A few of
the* YOUNG PEOPLE *are playful. They begin gesturing*

behind them as much as if to say, "Come on, here's a
funny old beggar." ASLAK *moves nearer to* PEER.]

ASLAK. [*Kindly yet queryingly.*] God be with you, old
friend.

PEER. [*Nodding at him.*] God be with you, Aslak.

ASLAK. [*Startled.*] You know me?

PEER. Your fame has spread far and wide. You once
fought with the devil.

ASLAK. [*Pleased.*] Think of that now.

PEER. So poor Mads Moen has turned up his toes. [*He
taps on the grave with his stick.*]

A YOUNG MAN. His friends are mourning. Everybody
loved him.

A YOUNG GIRL. He was a good man.

ASLAK. Aye, that he was. He had a forgiving heart.

ANOTHER YOUNG GIRL. He forgave even Peer Gynt.

PEER. Peer Gynt!

ASLAK. A fellow that stole his bride and ruined her long
ago. But Mads forgave him and married her.

A VOICE. And on his deathbed he prayed for Peer Gynt's
soul.

PEER. [*Standing up.*] He didn't!

ASLAK. Don't get excited, old man. He did.

PEER. A little brandy, good folks. [*He holds out his
hand, pinching the air with his fingers indicating alms.*

One of the YOUNG GIRLS *giggles and hides her face.* PEER
*looks at her with gaunt eyes, his face stricken. Then he
shakes his head as if driving the mood away and smiles.*]
It's true, I'm a little short of money today. But I've got
property. I'll sell some of it for a drink.

A BOY. [*Boldly.*] What you got to sell?

PEER. A lot of things—a palace for one thing.

BOY. Palace?

PEER. It's solidly built too.

ANOTHER LAD. I bid a button.

[*The* PEOPLE *enter into the fun for a moment. They
laugh.*]

PEER. [*Plaintively.*] At least you've got to bid the price
of a dram.

A GIRL. [*Calling out.*] He's a funny old duck.

PEER. [*Shouting out.*] Well then, who'll buy my horse?
Who bids for him? Peer Gynt used to ride him.

A VOICE. No, we don't need a horse.

ANOTHER VOICE. [*After a moment.*] What else you got
to sell?

PEER. Oh, a lot of things! How about some golden junk?
I bought it at a loss and I'll sell it at a loss.

ANOTHER VOICE. Gold? Let's see it.

PEER. [*Holding out his hat for alms.*] And a kingdom
to go with it.

A BOY. And a crown too?

PEER. Certainly a crown. It's made of the finest straw and'll fit any man who puts it on. [*Some of the people tap their foreheads and start moving away, satisfied they are dealing with an old lunatic.*] Hey, I've got more stuff to offer. Who'll buy some grey hair?—a madman's grey hair? [*He pulls at his hair as if offering them locks of it.*] And I've got a prophet's beard I'll sell. Think of it, the beard of a prophet. [*Plaintively.*] Where can I find rest and shelter?

ASLAK. [*Stepping up.*] In the village jail.

[*The* PEOPLE *laugh.*]

PEER. [*Humbly.*] Thank you kindly for your information.

ASLAK. There's a cell they fixed up for Peer Gynt once, but they never caught him.

PEER. Who was this remarkable man—Peer Gynt?

A MAN IN MOURNING. [*Turning back for an instant.*] A great liar.

A SECOND MAN. Nothing big ever happened that he didn't claim he'd done it. [*Gesturing to those that remain.*] But excuse me, friends. We have more important business. [*He turns and goes out, gesturing several* OTHERS *after him.*]

PEER. [*Piteously.*] And where is Peer Gynt now?

ASLAK. [*Who has remained.*] He ran away from the law and fled over the ocean. He was hanged a long time ago.

PEER. Hanged? I see.

ASLAK. He made his own bed and had to lie in it—stood in it, ha, ha.

[*He turns and moves on out and the rest of the* PEOPLE *follow him.* PEER *is left alone.*]

PEER. [*Calling after them.*] Thank you, boys and girls—and all you good people—for your kindness to me. [*He sits weakly down on the headstone, stares dully around him and leans heavily and forlornly on his stick.*] Religion and playing the fool may be all right, but a man's belly is the real voice. [*He scratches along the earth with his stick, finds something that interests him. He bends down and pulls it up.*] An onion. [*Chuckling.*] John the Baptist, they say, ate locusts and wild honey. I'm reduced to an onion. But then he was nothing but a preacher—and I—I'm an emperor. [*Shaking his head.*] You old fool prophet, you're no emperor, you're a—an onion. [*He sneezes, his eyes watering.*] And yes sir, old Peer Gynt, I'm going to peel you layer by layer. [*He plucks a layer off the onion and chews it.*] Tastes like Peer Gynt all right. [*He spits it out and goes on peeling.*] Ahah. Here's the fellow that dug for gold. Hmn. There's no juice in him if he ever had any. And here's a piece of rough hide with a hard edge. That must be when I was a fur trapper up there at Hudson's Bay. I was devilish tough then. [*Peering down at the onion.*] Here's something shaped like a crown—no thank you. [*He shudders and grimaces in sour remembrance.*] And here's the archeologist and here the prophet. [*He puts his finger to his nose.*] He stinks. He brings water to the eyes of an honest man. Here are two layers all rolled lovingly together. This is Peer Gynt living in pleasure and sin. And here is one with black streaks in it. Either the black cloth of a preacher or the skin of a Negro. [*He plucks several layers at the same time.*] What is an onion anyhow? Layer after layer. Where is the core, where is it—the onion's self? [*He breaks the rest of the onion apart.*] Damned if he's got any self. Right down to the center he's nothing but layers—smaller and smaller. [*Cynically.*] Nature is a joke.

[*He throws the remainder of the onion away and leans his head over on his stick again. Weariness and drowsiness enfold him. A strange aerial music begins in the air—*SOLVEIG'S *music. The scene slowly begins to fill with shadows in the foreground, and a radiance grows high up in the air at the rear. And there being born like a flower in this radiance, the vision of* SOLVEIG *again appears. She is carding wool in long rhythmic strokes and singing as she sits in her rocking chair. She is much older and frailer now.*]

SOLVEIG.
>   Dear love of mine come back to me soon.
>   Your burden is heavy alone
>   My love and my strength will share it with you
>   Solveig remembers, though you forget.

[PEER *springs to his feet, pale and aghast. The vision fades.*]

PEER. [*Muttering and shaking his head.*] There's nothing to remember—absolutely nothing.

[*He grabs up his old walking stick and starts hurriedly on out at the left front, but he stops suddenly for there in front of him stands the* BUTTONMOLDER.]

BUTTONMOLDER. Good evening, Peer Gynt!

PEER. [*Shivering and gasping weakly.*] The Button-molder?

BUTTONMOLDER. Exactly.

PEER. [*In horror.*] What do you want?

BUTTONMOLDER. I'm supposed to fetch you tonight.

PEER. Fetch me!

BUTTONMOLDER. You must go into my ladle—and be melted over again.

PEER. Melted!

BUTTONMOLDER. [*Shaking the ladle.*] It's all scrubbed clean and waiting. The Master sends orders to fetch your soul without delay.

PEER. [*Fervently, his voice high and pleading.*] Without warning—like this!

BUTTONMOLDER. [*As if quoting.*] And some were dancing and some were feasting when the summons came.

PEER. [*Tremulously.*] That's right—I read it in a book. My brain's in a whirl. You're— [*He points a shaky finger at the* BUTTONMOLDER.]

BUTTONMOLDER. You heard me—a Buttonmolder.

PEER. A rose by any other name. I know you—[*His voice almost a scream.*]—death!

BUTTONMOLDER. The statement's too bald. Retribution —what you will. But familiarly, between me and you, Peer Gynt—a Buttonmolder.

PEER. [*Lowers his head sorrowfully, then jerks it up*

again.] I am worth better treatment than this. I am not as bad as you think I am.

BUTTONMOLDER. [*Indulgently.*] That's not the question at all.

PEER. I've done a lot of good things here on earth, I have.

BUTTONMOLDER. That's not the question, either.

PEER. [*His voice has become unctuous, subservient and even sly.*] Maybe I've been a blunderer and failure in many ways, but I am not a hardened sinner.

BUTTONMOLDER. You are not a sinner at all in the deeper sense. So the Master will excuse you from the torment-ing pain— [*He clutches at his stomach with his free hand and shivers and shudders.*] And you'll land with the other scraps in the casting ladle.

PEER. Scraps!

BUTTONMOLDER. Use any name that you please—the im-pulse that fails, the flower that never blooms.

PEER. [*Beginning to get angry.*] You can't fool me. Call it a ladle or a burning lake of fire, hell and hereafter are all the same to sinners. It says so in the Scriptures. [*Shouting.*] Get away from me, Satan! Be off with you.

BUTTONMOLDER. [*Now unctuous and sly in his turn.*] No use getting angry like that. What has to be, has to be. You are yourself and nothing more and it is this self the Master sends for. You say you haven't been much of a sinner.

PEER. All in all, I have been a pretty good fellow. [*En-couraged.*] You seem like a reasonable gentleman.

BUTTONMOLDER. You haven't been much of an example of virtue—now have you? You wouldn't say your character is a thing of honor.

PEER. I guess I couldn't make much of a claim to that.

BUTTONMOLDER. So it's all clear. You are a sort of so-so —a nonentity. [*He lifts his ladle triumphantly.*]

PEER. You're wrong there, I am Peer Gynt. Peer Gynt, you hear me? And I have done big things in this world.

BUTTONMOLDER. So might a gnat say, from the gnat's point of view. Now if you'd been a really big sinner— gone after sinning on a grand scale—made your mark in the world.

PEER. Well, then I did. I've been a thoroughly bad fellow.

BUTTONMOLDER. Pooh, pooh. You took your sinning lightly. Always a wave of the hand and a good excuse for Number One.

PEER. [*Murmuring.*] Number One. That's me. I've been looking after that fellow all right. Who else would?

BUTTONMOLDER. [*Laughing.*] And he wasn't worth it. So the torturing sulphur pool is not for people like you, people who just splash in sin and spatter themselves a little. That's reserved for sinners with a conscience.

PEER. [*Quickly, affirmatively.*] Thank you then and I'll be going along.

[*He takes a step forward, but the* BUTTONMOLDER *stops him, sticking his ladle across as a bar in front of him.*]

BUTTONMOLDER. Oh, no you won't. You are to be melted over.

PEER. [*Now really angry.*] Stop this nonsense.

BUTTONMOLDER. Nonsense? You worked at ladling as a boy. You know often the moldings came out, well, frankly, like junk. The button was misshapen and without loops. What did you do when that happened?

PEER. I threw the junk away.

BUTTONMOLDER. But my Master is more economical. He throws nothing away as unusable. Maybe you were molded to be a shiny button on the vest of the world—who knows? But the loop failed. You were faulty, so you must go back into the scrap goods box to be molded over.

PEER. [*Incredulously.*] You mean you want to melt me up with any Tom, Dick and Harry into something new?

BUTTONMOLDER. [*Merrily.*] That's the idea—the way they do with a piece of money at the mint when the stamp's worn off.

PEER. Your Master is certainly a stingy fellow. [*Pleadingly.*] You've got to let me out of this. What is one button or a wornout penny to a man in your Master's position?

BUTTONMOLDER. It's the mortal value he's thinking of.

[*He opens the ladle top and slaps it shut again.*]

PEER. I'll not let you do it. I'll fight against you. I'll defend myself—tooth and claw, I'll—

BUTTONMOLDER. The same old Peer—he fights with his fists and hopes to win. Come now, be reasonable. You are not good enough for heaven and not bad enough for hell. You've got to be melted down.

PEER. [*In agony.*] I'm myself and nothing more—Peer

Gynt. And I won't give up one bit of myself to you or anybody else. [*Wiping the clammy sweat from his brow with his sleeve.*] Please, sir. Give me a little more time. Time is nothing to that Master of yours. Who knows, there might be an hour of redemption for me? I might come on happier days. [*Indicating his clothes.*] You've caught me unawares—in bad circumstance. [*The* BUTTONMOLDER *shakes his head.* PEER *almost sobs.*] To think of becoming a mote in the body of some crass stranger—a molding-ladle creature. The thought of it makes my soul puke.

BUTTONMOLDER. [*Touches him soothingly on the shoulder.*] Dear Peer, you needn't carry on so violently about such a little thing.

PEER. [*Throws up his hands bitterly.*] Such a little thing! You mean to wipe me out, take away my existence. You call that a little thing!

BUTTONMOLDER. We'll only make you over. What difference would it make in the scheme of things? After all, you have never existed.

PEER. [*Staring at him.*] Never existed! You make me laugh. [*Beating his breast.*] Look at me. Here I stand. Peer Gynt before you. I have grown old in experience. Never existed! What silly talk.

BUTTONMOLDER. I have my orders. Look, here it is written—"Fetch me Peer Gynt." [*He lifts the lid of the ladle and holds it up for* PEER *to see. There is a blinding light in the ladle and it shines in* PEER'S *face. He starts back with a sharp exclamation. The* BUTTONMOLDER *laughs and slaps the top of the ladle shut again.*] "He has been in opposition to his own life. Into the ladle he goes as faulty goods."

PEER. [*His teeth chattering.*] Does it really say Peer Gynt and not somebody else—'Rasmus or John maybe?

BUTTONMOLDER. Oh, I melted up 'Rasmus and John a long time ago. Come peacefully now.

[*He gestures and starts to lead* PEER *away, who seems for an instant pulled along as if by an invisible and over-powering force. Then his psychic rebellion surges into vehemence and energizes him. He moves stubbornly back.*]

PEER. I'll not do it. Who knows, tomorrow it might turn out you've got the wrong man. [*Shaking his cudgel at the* BUTTONMOLDER.] It is a big responsibility you take on yourself.

BUTTONMOLDER. [*Intrigued by* PEER'S *physical vehe-mence.*] But I have it before me in writing. [*He jiggles the ladle a bit.*]

PEER. [*Stamping the ground, then wheedling.*] You've got to give me a little time.

BUTTONMOLDER. I confess you are a likable fellow, after all. Such will power!

PEER. That's it! Will power. It carries a man through.

BUTTONMOLDER. What could you prove by the extra time?

PEER. [*Stoutly.*] I'd prove that my life has counted for something—that I've been myself all the days of my life.

I'd prove—well—I've existed—yes, I've been a really great sinner.

BUTTONMOLDER. How would you prove it?

PEER. [*Gesturing vaguely off.*] The way they do in the courts. I'd get witnesses and affidavits.

BUTTONMOLDER. [*Shaking his head.*] I'm afraid my Master will not accept them.

PEER. But they will be bona fide witnesses. Please, Buttonmolder—I can see you are a good fellow at heart. Let me borrow myself for a while. Allow me out on bail. A man can only be born once in this world—and it's wrong to wipe him out with no second chance.

BUTTONMOLDER. It would be a waste of the Master's time.

PEER. But he's got plenty of it to spare. [*Eagerly.*] Well, are we agreed then?

BUTTONMOLDER. [*Stares at* PEER *and finally smiles.*] It might be dramatic. I agree then. But remember, at the next crossroads we will meet again.

[*But his last words are wasted on* PEER *who has gone stomping swiftly out at the left front. The* BUTTON-MOLDER *stands chuckling and gazing after him. The light fades out.*]

PART TWO

Scene V

*A dark wooded hill where two roads meet.
Near the center of the scene is a signpost with
two signs pointing like lean sharp fingers down
their respective roads. At the foot of the post
is a squat gray boulder. Fogs and mist are rolling through the woods.* PEER *comes making his
way in from the right rear. He is trudging
along as if worn out from his great exertions
and journeyings among the hills.*

PEER. That's the way it is in this world. Need a good
word and you can't get it. Who would have thought a
witness would be so hard to find. Everywhere I go—
on the roads, in the villages—nobody knows me. They
have heard of me. Oh, sure, everybody's heard of Peer
Gynt. But he doesn't exist, they say. He's just a legend—
a folk-tale handed down. What a mess things are when
a man has to prove that he has ever lived!

[*He looks uncertainly at the sign and mops his forehead
with his sleeve. An* OLD BENT SKINNY FELLOW *with a
staff in his hand and a sack on his shoulder enters from
the left rear.*]

OLD MAN. [*In a plaintive wheedling voice.*] Please sir,
give a poor beggar a shilling.

PEER. [*Turns and looks at him. Testily.*] Sorry, I'm short of money myself.

OLD MAN. [*With a glad cry.*] Prince Peer! So we meet again.

[*He lurches over and grabs* PEER *in an embrace.* PEER *pulls angrily back from him.*]

PEER. Keep off.

OLD MAN. He doesn't remember the old man of the mountains.

PEER. Why, you can't be—

OLD MAN. The King of the Trolls.

PEER. [*Incredulously.*] The Troll King!

TROLL KING. I'm not what I used to be, Prince Peer.

PEER. I see that.

TROLL KING. I'm ruined—but not in the sense you ruined my daughter. I'm bankrupt. Stripped of everything and hungry as a hound.

PEER. [*Now embraces him in sudden joy.*] Hooray! I've found a witness—a true witness. [*Impatiently.*] I'm in a sort of bind and I've got to have a witness or an affidavit. You remember the night I came to your palace.

TROLL KING. Of course I do, Prince Peer.

PEER. Forget about this prince stuff. You remember, you wanted to cut me in my eye and make me over from Peer Gynt into a troll.

TROLL KING. [*Nodding agreement.*] And you were a stubborn fellow.

PEER. Yeh, that's right, stubborn. I stood on my own two feet, didn't I, and I wouldn't let you do it. I gave up honor and love and power—everything, just in order to remain Peer Gynt. Now that's what I want you to swear to.

TROLL KING. [*Quickly.*] I couldn't.

PEER. [*Sharply.*] Why not?

TROLL KING. Surely you won't force me to tell a lie. You're bound to remember that you put on the Troll tail and drank the mead.

PEER. [*Sternly.*] But I wouldn't marry the woman. I wouldn't do that.

TROLL KING. Because you'd already had your pleasure out of her.

PEER. That's a lie.

TROLL KING. And besides, when you left the palace, you had our slogan written behind your ear. You scratched it there.

[*He tries to get behind* PEER *and indicate the place on his skull, but* PEER *brushes him off.*]

PEER. I didn't.

TROLL KING. I can still see the markings of it—the doctrine—"Troll, to thyself be enough." [PEER *throws up his hands angrily.*] And all the days of your life you have lived according to that text. [*He points a skinny accusing finger at* PEER.] You have lived like a troll, but you kept the secret. It made you able to get on top of the world as a wealthy man. And now you come here trying to deny it. You're a great trickster, Peer, and I won't fall for it. Listen. [*Pulling a newspaper from his bag.*] Here you can see it in black and white—how the foreign press praises you—the *Journal* tells your success story and the *Times* describes you likewise—in the obituary column.

PEER. Obituary—but I'm not dead.

TROLL KING. You turned troll. It's all the same.

PEER. You'd better go to an asylum. You're mad.

[*He tries to push on by, but the* TROLL KING *clings to him.*]

TROLL KING. An asylum's what I'm hunting for. Do you know where I can find one? I have no friends any more. Nobody knows me. I'm a poor homeless beggar.

PEER. So am I for that matter. My princely self actually is in hock. [*Angrily.*] And it's the fault of you confounded trolls—the bad company I kept.

TROLL KING. And I thought you could help me. Goodby. I will try to work my way into the city.

PEER. [*Scathingly.*] Much good you'll do there.

TROLL KING. I'll try to get me a job as an actor. I see they are doing a lot of type casting these days. Or maybe I will write a farce—a wise and witty thing—on the national heritage—all about the group spirit and the new day. [*Waggling his hand in the air.*] Sic Transit Gloria Mundi.

[*He goes waddling off at the right rear.* PEER *looks after him. Gradually he sinks down on the boulder and gazes around him. His voice rises piteous and forlorn in self-accusation.*]

PEER. Well, Peer, your ship is wrecked. [*Staring about him at the valley mist.*] You must try to float on the pieces. [*Shaking his head.*] Fog, fog—everything vague and misty, like the inside of a white tomb—a sepulchre. They say Gabriel will blow his horn some day. He might as well blow it now. King Peer Gynt is finished. *Petrus Gyntus Caesar fecit!* * What's that? Like children crying? Like singing too. And here come yarn balls tumbling at my feet. [*He springs up in terror and kicks about him in the fog.*] Get away from me! Let me alone!

BALLS OF YARN. [*Like little children on the ground.*]
>   We are the thoughts
>   You should have thought.
>   Little legs
>   You should have got.

PEER. I've been a father all right—but my brat was a monster with a crooked leg.

BALLS OF YARN.
>   Up we would soar
>   In clamorous calls
>   But here we must roll
>   As grey yarn balls.

PEER. [*Striking at the fog with his stick.*] You confounded rascal! So you are trying to trip your father up. [*He stands listening. The wind starts swirling the fog about, and stray autumn leaves begin tumbling by, borne along the currents of air.* PEER *hits at the leaves and calls*

* NOTE: If necessary, this scene can be cut from here to where Peer sees the falling star.

out sardonically to them.] Withered autumn leaves falling on me now— Dead hopes, dead hopes, where are you flying?

WITHERED LEAVES. [*In a sighing chant.*]
>We are the proverb
>You should have obeyed,
>But see how your trifling
>Has hurt and betrayed.
>
>The worm has gnawed us
>And eaten us through,
>And never our fruit
>To ripening grew.

PEER. [*Angrily.*] Quit bellyaching. Leaves can still serve as good fertilizer.

A WITHERED LEAF. [*Whispering in the air.*]
>We are sweet songs—
>You should have sung us.
>A thousand times
>You have crushed and wrung us.
>
>In the hollow of your heart
>We lay and waited.
>With choking poison
>Now your throat is sated.

PEER. Stupid poison!—Stupid songs! [*He throws up his hands and turns toward the signpost. He notices the dew drops hanging there in a row and points his stick at them.*] Ho, you dew drops—winking at me with your little eyes.

DEW DROPS. [*In quick elfin voices.*]
　　　　We are the tears
　　　　You never shed.
　　　　Ice spears to pierce
　　　　Could melt instead.

　　　　Now the spear sticks
　　　　In the shaggy breast
　　　　The wound is closed
　　　　And our power is passed.

PEER. [*Strikes the signpost sharply with his cudgel.*]
That's the end of you, raindrops. Now you're only dirty
water soaking in the earth. [*He sinks down on the boulder by the signpost. Reaching over he pulls up a handful
of straws and breaks them. He stares at them.*] A handful of straw—a lot of little resolutions—twisted together
in a single life.

[*He twists the straws together. As if hurt, they let out
little tiny whistling notes—E-flat, F-sharp and G.* PEER
*throws the straws violently from him, bowing his head
helplessly over in his hands. The twisted straws lie in a
little pool of light, glimmering there.*]

STRAWS. [*In their shrill unison.*]
　　　　We are the deeds
　　　　You should have done
　　　　But doubt has smothered
　　　　Us everyone.

　　　　On judgement day
　　　　We will fly to heaven,
　　　　And you'll lie lost
　　　　And unforgiven.

PEER. Leave me then. Fly on to your heaven! [*His shoulders shake with sudden sobs.*] Not even a reed to lean on—nothing but broken straws. [*He controls his sobs and wipes his eyes. Across the sky at the rear a falling star shoots with a streamer of flame.* PEER *looks at it and takes off his hat somewhat in awe and speaks gently and brokenly.*] Peer Gynt sends you greetings, Brother Falling Star. You have lighted your little hour and gone out in a yawn. [*He yawns and stands up a moment. Then he suddenly screams out in the silence.*] Is there nobody anywhere—nobody in the whole universe! No one in heaven or hell to help me! [*He falls down on his knees, his voice rising in an agony of half-sobbing soliloquy.*] Help me, help me! Somebody—where are you! But there is no one—no one. So poor can a soul become—so lonely when he goes back into nothingness, into the foggy emptiness. [*Kissing the ground.*] Oh, sweet and wonderful earth. Don't be angry with me, forgive me that I trampled your grass so uselessly with my heavy feet. [*He strokes the ground with his hands, then lifts his gnarled and weatherbeaten face.*] You sweet and glorious sun. You have wasted your shining on me. You have made the hut warm and happy, but it has been empty. The owner of this house was never at home. Oh, wonderful sun and wonderful earth, forgive me. You lighted my mother to no purpose, for I was conceived in the dark. And my birth was a penalty to be paid with my life. Let me go away, let me hide myself in the mountains. And there let the snow be piled high above me and a signboard on top with words that say, "Here lies nobody." And after that then—well, the rest is nothing.

[*His voice dies wearily out. Far in the distance church*

bells start ringing and then people's voices are **heard**
singing from the valley below.]

PEOPLE'S VOICES. [*Mingled with the bells.*]
> Blessed morning when the tongues
> Of the kingdom of God
> Struck earth like flaming steel—
> From earth toward the castle
> Now the inheritor sings
> In the tongue of
> The Kingdom of God.

PEER. [*Springs up in terror. Shrieking.*] The bells, the
church bells! [*In a great troll voice.*] Come away!
Away—y! [*With the outlandish movements of a troll
he runs howling away at the left rear, his howl echoing
through the mountains. The scene fades out.*]

PART TWO

Scene VI

High up in the rugged mountains. In the shadow at the back the little pioneer cabin is dimly discerned with its reindeer antlers still up above the door. PEER *comes in from the left rear. He is talking to himself in a wavering monologue, but trying to recapture a touch of his sardonic humor.*

PEER. Your time is running out, Peer Gynt, no doubt of that. And the shoe is beginning to pinch—to blister in fact. [*Grimly as he blinks about him.*] I'm no Napoleon, that's certain. He didn't need witnesses to prove he existed. He left his mark on the world.

BUTTONMOLDER. [*Comes in at the left front. Calling out.*] Where are the affidavits of your sins, Peer Gynt? [*Without turning around,* PEER *shakes his head.*] I see you haven't got them, let's get started.

PEER. I'd like to ask you a simple question.

BUTTONMOLDER. Proceed.

PEER. I'll come straight to the point. What is it to be one's self, actually?

BUTTONMOLDER. To be one's self is to destroy the worser self.

PEER. Still the wretched moralist.

BUTTONMOLDER. Man must always strive to learn what the Master means—him to be.

PEER. [*Dully.*] But suppose a man never found out what he was meant to be?

BUTTONMOLDER. He must feel it by intuition.

PEER. [*Frustrated.*] Intuition!

BUTTONMOLDER. But we waste time. You missed your calling, so come along.

PEER. What was my calling?

BUTTONMOLDER. A man must first conquer himself before he finds out. You didn't, so you failed to exist. Come.

PEER. But I've had existence, I tell you. I have been a dreadful sinner.

BUTTONMOLDER. Don't start that all over again.

PEER. [*Volubly.*] I mean a really great sinner. Not just in deeds, but in desires and words. I've lived a damnable life.

BUTTONMOLDER. A trifling matter.

PEER. Remember, I sold Negro slaves.

BUTTONMOLDER. Others sell minds and hearts.

PEER. I sent Hindu idols to China.

BUTTONMOLDER. Effort wasted.

PEER. [*Vehemently.*] I played at being prophet.

BUTTONMOLDER. Prophets usually end up in the casting ladle.

PEER. And I believed in fate, not God.

BUTTONMOLDER. Fate is only God in the past tense. [*Sharply.*] Time's up.

PEER. [*Ragingly.*] Everything is up. The owl smells the daylight. Don't you hear him hooting?

[*In the distance the church bells begin ringing, followed by faraway singing.* PEER *shrinks away from the sound as if his ears were sensitive and hurt by it and draws closer to the* BUTTONMOLDER. *The* BUTTONMOLDER *takes him by the arm.*]

BUTTONMOLDER. The people are going to church. You and I go another way.

PEER. [*Pointing.*] Look, what's shining there.

BUTTONMOLDER. Only a light in a house.

PEER. [*Quaveringly.*] Who is that singing?

[SOLVEIG'S *voice is heard in the background, tender, lyric and ethereal.*]

BUTTONMOLDER. Only the song of some woman.

[*The singing of the* PEOPLE *continues in the distance. The outlines of the little house now come clearer to view.* PEER *stands there listening to* SOLVEIG'S *voice, thoughts beating in his fermenting mind. His eyes light on an axe leaning against the steps to the little house. He pulls loose from the* BUTTONMOLDER.]

PEER. My axe! My little house! Solveig's kept them for me. Listen, she's singing. [*He runs over and picks up the axe. He stares at it, feels it with his hand and turns to the* BUTTONMOLDER *in angry jubilance, pointing the helve at the little house.*] Fool that I have been! There is the witness I wanted. Solveig. She can swear to my sins.

[*The little hut at the rear becomes still clearer.*]

BUTTONMOLDER. [*Loudly.*] Too late, the summons is served.

PEER. It is not too late. Get away. If your ladle were as big as a coffin, it still couldn't hold me and all of my sins. She will prove it to you. [*He draws closer to the house as the* BUTTONMOLDER *remains suddenly silent watching him.*] Go around said the Voice, but I can't do that now. Straight through all these wishes and appetites to her. And so let her damn me to salvation. [*He shudders and then turns sharply away from the steps of the little house, feeling the axe with his hand as if for comfort.*] But what right have I to ask her to judge me!

BUTTONMOLDER. True. What right?

[*He chuckles grimly and sardonically. The song in the house rises audibly again,* PEER *pulls off his old hat, lifts his bearded and time-scarred visage and straightens his shoulders, holding the axe tight in his grasp.*]

PEER. Tighten your belt, Peer. Face the music. [*He runs up the steps. At the same moment* SOLVEIG *comes out on the little porch illuminated in the light. She is dressed in dark clothes for church and carries the little white hymn book of her youth in one cotton-gloved hand. She supports her frailty with a staff in the other. She stops and stares through her spectacles down at* PEER *who starts back from her with a groan. He looks toward the* BUTTONMOLDER *who waits with the ladle stuck up beside him like a spear, implacable, unyielding.* PEER *flings himself down on the steps and cries out in a loud voice.*] Denounce me to this fellow. Give judgement on me, a sinner!

SOLVEIG. [*Incredulous, tremulous, murmuring.*] Peer, Peer! Praise be to God, he's home at last. [*She stretches out her hymn book over him.*]

PEER. [*Wildly.*] Tell him how sinfully I have treated you these long years.

[SOLVEIG *takes a step toward him as he shudders and shrinks away from her.*]

SOLVEIG. You have not treated me sinfully, my lad.

[PEER *throws up his hand in a gesture of hopelessness and flings himself backward on the steps.* SOLVEIG *slowly and with the aid of her cane sinks down beside him.*]

BUTTONMOLDER. [*Satirically.*] A witness, a witness, Peer Gynt!

PEER. [PEER'S *voice rises in anguished pleading to* SOL-VEIG.] Scream out my guilt!

[SOLVEIG *is now kneeling on the floor. She reaches her hand over and touches* PEER'S *forehead. Another groan breaks from him.*]

SOLVEIG. [*Blissful, devotional.*] You have made my whole life a wonderful song. [*A great tired sigh goes out of* PEER.] Bless you for coming home again. Bless you for this morning meeting.

PEER. [*Sepulchrally and with the despair of the damned.*]
I am lost.

[*He rises and comes blindly down the steps to give over
to the* BUTTONMOLDER. *The music of the unseen church
people grows stronger, then subsides.*]

SOLVEIG. [*Rising and moving down the steps.*] Lost!

PEER. Eternally damned. [*To the* BUTTONMOLDER.] I'm
ready. [*He takes the* BUTTONMOLDER'S *arm.*]

SOLVEIG. [*Comes over to him.*] We'll go in. The fire will
burn bright and warm will you be.

PEER. [*Loudly.*] And at the last—death! Death as it was
meant to be. I must go down into the foggy land. [*Anguished.*] But never to have lived—never to have really
struggled and won! My dreams vanished, my loud talking hushed! Whimperings and baby cries in a senseless
jungle! To live and never exist. To exist and never live.
The farce is ended.

SOLVEIG. [*Gently.*] But you have lived, my dearest one.

PEER. I am too weak for riddles.

SOLVEIG. A beautiful shining life.

PEER. I could answer the Sphinx, but not you.

SOLVEIG. [*Serene.*] And now you are home, safe home.
Come.

PEER. There is my home, in the ladle. I'm one of life's
misshapen buttons—to be melted down.

BUTTONMOLDER. At last you are a sensible fellow, Peer
Gynt.

SOLVEIG. [*Simply, with certainty.*] Our life is *now* beginning.

PEER. Can a man be born again when he is old?

SOLVEIG. [*Smiling.*] Yes.

PEER. [*Staring at her.*] Yes, she says in her wisdom. Once she was simple and like a child. Tell me where has Peer Gynt been since you saw him last?

SOLVEIG. Been?

PEER. [*Angrily.*] Yes, been—with the mark of destiny on him—a troll text behind his ear?

SOLVEIG. [*Smiling.*] That riddle's easy.

PEER. Where was I, the real self? Not that quack emperor and slave dealer and braggart stuff? But me, Peer Gynt—with the stamp of God on my brow that lied when it said I was a man? [*He hits his forehead with his fist.*]

SOLVEIG. Safe with me.

PEER. Safe?

SOLVEIG. In my faith, in my hope and in my love.

PEER. [*With a cry.*] What do you say! Stop it! Stop it!

SOLVEIG. Like my unborn child—inside me—here—[*She touches her heart.*]

PEER. [*Keeps staring at her. Murmuring strangely.*] The lad inside you—me?

SOLVEIG. [*Nods.*] Waiting, waiting to be born. [*Her face shining.*] In my memory, in my heart you have lived.

PEER. [PEER'S *face begins breaking and working in emotion. Something of the light of love shines suddenly out over that tumultuous heaving, must as the light of the setting—or the rising—sun shining over a wave-rolling and tumultuous ocean. He falls on his knees and cries out in a mystic affirmation, hugging her to him.*] Innocent woman—my mother, my wife! [*Sobbing with joy.*] You have saved me.

SOLVEIG. It's I that am saved.

PEER. —By your love. [*He continues sobbing, holding her close.*]

BUTTONMOLDER. [*Angrily.*] I did not foresee this.

PEER. [*Loudly, affirmatively.*] My empire was here. I have found myself. [*He grasps his axe and rises from the ground, his arm around* SOLVEIG.]

BUTTONMOLDER. [*Disgusted.*] My Master should have warned me of this possibility. [*He flings his ladle across his shoulder and marches stiffly and offendedly off at the right, calling back.*] Beware lest we meet at the last cross-roads, Peer Gynt!

[*But* PEER GYNT *has already turned toward the house with* SOLVEIG. *He shakes his head emphatically without looking around. Hand in hand the two go up the steps. The singing of the unseen people and the ringing of the church bells swell loudly and triumphantly in, sending their benediction over the scene and over the two now moving toward the life that waits for them—the richest life of all. A radiance is on the little door as it opens of its own will before them. They go sweetly in and it closes behind them. The singing and the bells grow louder.*]

THE END

No. 1 - OPENING FLUTE SOLO - Old Folk Melody

No. 2 - SOLVEIG'S THEME

Slow

The win-ter will come and the spring go by, The sum-mer and long au-tum

too. But some day you'll come - I know you will come. And I'll wait for you as I

said I would. - (Humming _)

_ -)

Part I - Sc.1 - No.3 - ON THE WAY TO THE WEDDING - Norwegian Folk Tune

Part I - Sc.2 - No.4 - WEDDING DANCE (1) - Norwegian Folk Tune

Part I - Sc. 2 - No. 5 - WEDDING DANCE (2) - Norwegian Folk Tune

Part I - Sc. 4 - No. 6 - DANCE OF THE TROLLS - Norwegian Folk Tune

Part I - Sc. 6 - No. 7 - Chant - MAN THAT IS BORN OF WOMAN = from the "Evangelical Psalmist"

Man that is born of Woman
Is of few days and full of trouble
He cometh forth like a flower

And is cut down
He fleeth also as a shadow
And continueth not.

Part I - Sc. 1 - No. 8 - LUTE MUSIC - from E. Yafil

Part II - Sc. 2 - No. 9 - SONG OF THE DROWSY ARAB WARRIORS - from E. Yafil

Part II - Sc. 2 - No. 10 - ANITRA'S DANCE - with her Maidens -   from E. Yafil

Part II - Sc.2 - No.11 - PEER'S SONG TO ANITRA

He barred the door of par - a - dise and took the key a -

long The north wind bore him out to sea While love - ly

wom- en all for - lorn, wept on the o - cean strand.

Part II - Sc. 4 - No.12 - Chant - BLESSED IS THE MAN "from the Evangelical Psalmist"

Blessed is the man that walketh not in the counsel of the un-godly. Nor standeth in the way of sinners, nor sitteth in the seat of the scornful. But his delight is in the law of the Lord. And in his law doth he meditate day and night. And he shall be like a tree planted by the rivers of water that bringeth forth his fruit in his season. His leaf also shall not wither. And whatso-ever he doeth shall prosper. The un-godly are not so. But are like the chaff which the wind driveth away.

Part II - Sc.4 - No.13 - FUNERAL HYMN - 13th Cent. English

what shall I frail man be plead - ing, who for me be

in - ter - ced - ing, when the just are mer - cy need - ing. King of

maj - es - ty tre - men- dous who dost free sal - vat - ion send us

Fount of pit - y then be - friend us.

Part II - Sc. 5 - No.14 - Chant - BLESSED MORNING - from the "Evangelical Psalmist"

Blessed Morning when the tongues
Of the Kingdom of God
Struck earth like flaming steel
From earth towards the castle
Now the inheritor sings
In the tongue of the Kingdom of God

167